Running Your Own

TYPING SERVICE

Running Your Own

TYPING

SERVICE

Doreen Huntley

Kogan Page
WORKING
for
YOURSELF
Series

First published in Great Britain in 1987
by Kogan Page Ltd
120 Pentonville Road
London N1 9JN

British Library Cataloguing in Publication Data
Huntley, Doreen
    Running your own typing service. — (The Kogan
    Page working for yourself series)
    1. Typewriting services   2. Home-based businesses
    I. Title
    651.3'741   Z49.A2

    ISBN 1-85091-242-4

Printed and bound in Great Britain
by Biddles Ltd, Guildford

Contents

To 'Waffle' and 'Cough' without whom
this book could not have been written

Introduction

Running a typing service must be one of the easiest ways to make money at home. The business can be as small, or as large, as you like; it can be fitted around the needs of housework/children, full- or part-time employment and other commitments and, once established, can provide a useful regular income for relatively little outlay.

This practical guide – written by a successful 'home-typist' – sets out to show how typing skills can be cheaply and easily put to use in the setting up and running of a small home-based business. Later chapters show how to cope as your business grows, how to expand and develop your service and, ultimately, how to set up your own secretarial agency. You have already taken the first essential step by seeking advice and information. So many small businesses fail simply through lack of preliminary planning. The time spent thinking about the service you wish to offer, how best to market it and what your commitment is going to be, can make all the difference between success and failure.

Who can run a typing service?

Nowadays many skilled typists find themselves out of work for one reason or another – the advent of children, disability, retirement, redundancy, and so on. Although the vast majority of these are likely to be women, a growing proportion of men are trained in keyboard skills and office practice and there is no reason why they should not be just as successful in running their own typing service as the more traditional female typist. Provided you have, or can acquire, the necessary basic skills, own (or can hire) a typewriter and can organise yourself effectively, you can run a typing service.

You don't need to be out of work to operate a small home-based typing service. One full-time college librarian in the north takes in 'overflow' typing from other home-typists and agencies (as well as the occasional dissertation from the students at her college) as and when she feels like it. In this way she has acquired a small, fairly

9

regular, part-time income for very little outlay. In one sense you could say she is 'testing the water' (and her abilities as a businesswoman) without losing the security of a full-time job. When she retires in a few years' time she intends to establish a small home-typing service of her own which will supplement her pension and occupy her spare time.

Two young ladies who, after acquiring all the necessary secretarial skills at college, found that they could not get the kind of jobs they wanted, formed a partnership, bought a word processor (one of them already owned a typewriter) and started a business in a bedroom of their flat. After several months of hard work and determined marketing their word-processing business took off. Eighteen months later they decided to open a secretarial agency and they haven't look back since.

Between these two extremes are the many women (and men) who are somewhat restricted in the number of hours they have available for work – the housewife with children at school, the new mother with children at home, the part-time worker with hours to spare, the student wishing to work during the long summer holidays, and so on. Whoever you are and whatever your circumstances you can, with a little luck, plenty of common sense and lots of enthusiastic determination, run a successful home-typing service.

Who needs home-typists?

Typing is a skill that is always needed by someone somewhere. Polytechnic, college and university students are required to submit typewritten theses and dissertations, so if you live near one of these institutions, your services are likely to be in great demand. Many small businesses cannot afford their own clerical staff and will often be delighted to have someone to prepare invoices, accounts and letters etc. If you live in a rural area you may find that business people and farmers will be pleased to have typing work done locally. Clubs and societies need people to type up minutes, agendas, annual accounts, circulars and so forth, and larger organisations often have overflow typing work (especially legal drafts and accounts). You may be able to offer services to the general public, such as the presentation and typing of curricula vitae and correspondence; writers' and drama groups, which can be found in virtually every town, often need someone to type up their members' manuscripts and plays.

Your chances of success are obviously higher if you live in a town or city, within reasonable access of a college or university, and are within easy reach of the town centre (by car or bus). However, don't despair if you live in a rural area. If you can provide a good service at a cheaper rate than people would pay for taking their typing business to the nearest town then you could be on to a winner. Home-typing has potential as a service by mail too, and you could develop that aspect.

What will it involve?

Apart from brushing up your typing skills and acquiring essential start-up equipment you will need to find out what demand there is for home-typing in your area and plan an appropriate marketing strategy. You will find information about start-up equipment needs in Chapters 1 and 6; Chapter 2 includes a section on assessing the demand in your area and Chapter 5 offers advice on marketing your service.

Depending on your particular circumstances and aspirations, you may need to raise capital in order to purchase equipment and supplies (though a typing service *can* be started on a shoe-string) and you will need to organise an area in your home which you can use almost exclusively for your work.

There are also certain legal requirements, no matter how small your business, but these are relatively straightforward and should not cause any problems if you deal with them at the start. Chapter 3 provides a comprehensive coverage of the formal aspects of starting a business.

How far do you need to commit yourself?

The amount of time and effort involved in running a typing service really depends on how much *you* want to put in. The beauty of a home-based typing service is its flexibility (especially once you have built up a good supply of customers). You can adjust your work-load to suit your own commitments and income needs. Your involvement and commitment can range from negligible outlay and a few hours' work per week in your own home right through to opening your own secretarial agency with premises, staff and full-time work-load.

There really are no hard and fast rules about how much of your time, effort and capital should go into your typing service, although you shouldn't expect to make a lot of money from it if you are not prepared to work regularly (and sometimes at unsocial hours), meet deadlines and put in the effort required to keep good customers coming back. You *can* make money by typing on a 'now and then' basis, but it will not be very much, and it cannot be relied upon. If you want a more substantial, regular, income then you must be prepared to put in a lot more effort, especially in the first year when your business is establishing itself.

Your chances of success

Every year thousands of new small businesses are started up and most of them, sadly, fail. In the case of home-based typing services the most common causes of failure include lack of preliminary research, inadequate advertising, insufficient forethought about the service offered and how the business will be run, and poor costing. Another factor, often overlooked, is the level of enjoyment you get out of running your typing service. You will never make a great success out of any business if you are doing it solely for the financial gain – you must *like* doing it. However, the most important factor of all is your own determination to succeed.

The first year is usually the most critical in terms of success or failure. Many typing services that might have developed into very successful enterprises fail because their initiator loses heart at the lack of instantaneous success. Any business needs time to develop and a typing service (especially a small or part-time concern) is no exception. The initial flush of enthusiasm in setting up the office and putting out a few advertisements may soon dwindle when results seem to be negligible. This stage is almost universal in business start-ups, but if you follow the advice given in this book and elsewhere and have the appropriate skills and personal attributes, there is no reason why *your* business should not be a success.

Chapter 1

Look Before You Leap

This chapter is to help you decide whether or not running a typing service is really for you. You probably wouldn't be reading this book if you didn't already think it was, but before you skip straight on to Chapter 2, do at least consider some of the points raised.

Although setting up and running a typing service can be very rewarding, lucrative and interesting *it is not easy*. The ability to type 60 words per minute and answer the telephone will not, on its own, enable you to run a successful typing service. You will need to have a confident, outgoing personality, the ability to make decisions, meet deadlines and cope under stress. You will also need to be able to communicate well with people both in person and on the telephone – potential customers may be put off if you sound vague or unsure of yourself. Most important of all, you must be a self-starter. You will not have a boss or supervisor to tell you what to do – *you* will be your own boss. Don't make the mistake of expecting that your customers will treat you as an employee – they won't. The majority will expect *you* to take the lead in asking questions, ascertaining their precise needs, providing information, setting (or negotiating) deadlines and organising the actual work. So you must be able to make your own work-plan and stick to it. It will be up to you to decide how much work to take on, how much to charge, how long you think it will take to complete – and then actually sit down and get it done before your customer returns to collect it.

Are you the type?

Are you the sort of person who is going to cope well with, even thrive on, self-employment? The self-assessment questions below aim to help you find out. Only *you* can know how realistically you answer these – there's no point in trying to fool yourself!

Don't be too put off if you feel inexperienced or unsure. Although running a typing service is very much like running any other small business, the risks involved are usually quite a lot lower. This is especially true if you are not the main breadwinner in the family and are not investing a large amount of capital. You can often afford to learn as you go along; there's no reason why you shouldn't give it a go: you have very little to lose if you later find that it really is not for you. However, if you are more serious about making your service a success and if your success or failure is of some financial importance, *do* consider the following points very carefully before you decide to take the plunge.

Dealing with other people

How do you feel about other people in general? Do you usually enjoy meeting new people, or are you happier with people you know well and rather unsure of yourself with strangers?

Running a typing service usually involves a highly contrasted mix of working for hours on end on your own (or with your partner if you have one) interspersed with visits from customers (many of whom will quite happily spend hours of your valuable time chatting to you if you let them) and dealing with telephone calls. You will need to be very adaptable – happy both to work alone for long periods and to interact cheerfully with your customers when necessary.

Adaptability

Are you generally easygoing, happy to accept the status quo and rather upset when changes occur, or are you eager for new challenges, ready to adapt and learn new skills?

If you plan to cater for the particular demand in your area, you will almost certainly have to learn new skills and/or adapt to seasonal changes. You will be working for many different people, all of whom will have very different ideas about how they want their typing done. Small businesses usually require invoices, estimates, accounts, letters and mail shots whereas a writers' society may require you to type up several screenplays and manuscripts a year, and your local university may generate a seasonal flood of dissertations and theses. Unless you specialise (and you would be well advised to ensure that there is a sufficient market for your specialism before you start) you will need to have, or acquire, the ability to deal with many different kinds of typing assignment.

You will also need the ability to switch off from one task at short notice and switch on to another. You will not be able to ascertain, or remember, the requirements of the new customer who has just arrived at your door with a batch of invoices for typing if your mind is still at your desk constructing a CV for the previous one!

Industriousness and application

When you have a job to do, do you generally put it off until the last minute? Do you work well on routine tasks but find it difficult to get on with more demanding jobs, or do you find you can't settle if you know you have something to do and feel a great satisfaction in doing the job well?

Running a typing service is like running any other business – if you don't produce the goods as required, and when, your business will not last long. You must be able to apply yourself to the work you have taken on. Inevitably, some of it will seem either dreadfully routine and boring or so demanding it's difficult to know where to start. If you are normally able to set yourself goals in terms of getting work done, and almost always achieve these, you should have little difficulty.

Putting ideas into practice and making decisions

Are you generally unimaginative, preferring to follow the lead of others; occasionally inspired with a good idea but rarely bothering to carry it out; or generally resourceful, inventive and able to put ideas into practice? Do you find it difficult to make decisions of your own? Perhaps you are happier to take orders than to give them? Or do you usually find it easy to make, and act on, your own decisions?

One of the major factors affecting the success or failure of this type of business is the ability to 'get moving', to put good ideas into practice. Being your own boss means that *you* have to be able to manage your business, *you* have to make the plans, do the research, buy the equipment, deal with the customers, make sure the work gets done, and get the money in. Having a good idea is not enough. You must be able to make it work.

You must also feel confident in your own ability to make and follow through your own decisions. If you are too easily put off, or diverted by other people's advice and criticism, you will never get your ideas off the ground. In addition, you will often have to make rapid decisions during your working day – do you take on the extra work from the new customer who may provide a lot of regular work in the future and work overtime that evening to get it done; or do you turn him away because you have other commitments and feel your business can survive without his custom? Either way, the ability actually to *make* the decision, hopefully the right one, is just as important as the decision itself. If

15

you haver and mumble you will not only run the risk of putting your customer off for good, but of making the wrong decision (for you) as well. Planning in advance and having clear objectives (see below) will make day-to-day and long-term decision-making easier.

Planning, forecasting and organising
Are you generally poor at planning in advance, tending to make decisions on the spur of the moment when the need arises? Or are you generally a good organiser, far-sighted, able to plan in detail and then follow that plan through?

A major skill in the successful running of any small business is the ability to plan for both the long and short term. To begin with, your long-term goal may simply be to get your business off the ground but later, when your business begins to take off, you will find it easier to deal with problems such as work-overflow and the need for expansion if you have planned appropriately in advance. It is worth spending some time *before* you start up your business deciding what action you will take to achieve your aims. This means that you first have to *specify* your aims in terms of the financial reward required, the hours you wish to work per week, when you plan to take holidays etc, and then decide how best you can achieve these goals. You will also need to be a good organiser, both of yourself and others, if you are effectively to plan your day-to-day work schedule and carry it out. You must be able to assign priorities to your work-load, decide on a daily plan of action and carry it out effectively.

Delegation and dealing with subordinates and colleagues
If your business grows you may need to consider going into partnership, subcontracting or taking on staff. Hence the ability to organise and motivate others, as well as the ability to delegate responsibility, are also very necessary. Do you feel competent in dealing with subordinates? Can you give instructions with authority but without intimidation? Could you deal with unsavoury tasks such as disciplining staff or giving notice?

Determination and flexibility
When faced with a difficult task do you tend to become disheartened if you can't achieve your aims quickly? Do you persevere for a while but find other things begin to take priority, or do you enjoy the challenge and almost always complete the task to your own satisfaction?

You will never achieve success with your typing service if, once you have set your goals, you do not have the will-power to plough ahead regardless of minor crises and problems. This does not mean that you must never reconsider or learn from your experiences. As well as the determination to succeed and the will-power to keep going under pressure, you must retain a flexible attitude which will allow you to change your plans in the light of new opportunites or altered circumstances.

Coping under stress

Running a typing service almost inevitably involves periods when you are overloaded with work and other times when you are barely ticking over. It is all too easy to underestimate the time required to complete a piece of work and, especially if you are working from home, the additional pressures of other commitments (family, friends, housework and so on) can cause great stress. Some of these aspects are considered under 'Working from home' later in this chapter.

Remember that most self-employed people necessarily work very hard, long hours, and have to cope with the responsibility for the success or failure of their business 24 hours a day. Many people find it invigorating and inspiring to work under pressure whereas others find it extremely distressing. How do you cope with minor stresses? Are you inclined to make mountains out of molehills? Do you usually give up when things get too much for you, or are you generally able to see things in perspective, make an extra effort under pressure and cope well when the going gets tough?

Skills and abilities

The skills and abilities you need will, to some extent, be dictated by the kind of service you wish to offer. If you are going to set yourself up as a comprehensive word-processing/computerised data service for small businesses you will obviously be using a different range of skills from those necessary for the operation of a mobile secretarial service. Don't feel you have to restrict your service to the expertise you already possess – be prepared to extend your skills and learn new techniques. After all, the wider the service you can offer, the more custom you are likely to attract.

Clearly, there are certain skills you cannot do without – the ability to type accurately and reasonably fast being the obvious one. If you cannot type, or if it is some years since you did any typing and you need to brush up your skills, there are several ways of reaching the necessary standard. Your local education authority will almost certainly run classes in typing and office skills in your area, as may the Manpower Services Commission, and there are now numerous private agencies offering short, intensive courses in typing and word-processing. Check in your local newspaper or enquire at your library for details. If you cannot attend a course it *is* possible to teach yourself to type using a self-teaching manual (there are several available from bookshops and libraries and some are listed in Chapter 13); if you are purchasing a word processor or computer, you can use a typing-tutor program. This is a computer program which runs on your computer or word processor giving instructions and monitoring your progress as you go.

If possible, give preference to a course that teaches touch typing rather than one that requires you to look at the keyboard – you will be able to proceed faster and with fewer mistakes if you can acquire this skill. Touch typing takes longer to learn but is well worth it in terms of time saved later on. You should aim to achieve a typing speed of 50 words per minute (wpm) or more. Your course tutor or manual will tell you how to calculate your speed if you are unsure. Typing is a very labour intensive business, the cost of materials being much less than that of the labour input, so a significant proportion of your income per job is to cover the *time* you spend doing it (however you ultimately choose to charge). Therefore, if your typing speed is significantly slower than 50 wpm you will either have to charge more and risk losing work to your competitors, or accept a lower rate of pay because you will be working longer hours for the same financial reward.

As well as the ability to type, you will need a good understanding of grammar, punctuation and spelling. Many of your customers (business people and college students seem to be the worst culprits) will expect you to correct their mistakes. If your command of English is especially good you could even offer this as part of your service although in general your customers will expect you to correct spelling as a matter of course.

You will also need a fairly extensive knowledge of the various layouts and formats used in typing. To some extent this will depend on how much you intend to specialise (if at all). If you specialise, say, in typing up legal drafts, you will obviously need a *very* good understanding of the particular format involved whereas, if your service is more comprehensive, you will need a more general knowledge of how to lay out and present different kinds of material. Although some customers will tell you exactly how they want their typing laid out, many will expect *you* to explain the various styles available and advise them on the most suitable for their needs. (Having some samples to show them is useful.) Examples of some basic layouts of various typing assignments are included in the Appendix. Typing manuals will give you a broader view of the variety of formats you could use.

Should you wish to extend you service *beyond* that of straightforward typing, you will need to possess or acquire the relevant skills involved. Some of the additional services you might like to consider are outlined in Chapter 9. It is often the case that by offering a special service (such as an audio-typing facility for businessmen on the move) you can attract custom that would otherwise pass you by.

Finally, don't restrict yourself to the knowledge you already possess. Be prepared to learn new skills, at classes, at home, or even from your customers! If you can type you can learn to operate a word processor; if you can add you can learn to do simple bookkeeping. The more skills you possess, the greater choice you will have in operating your service and the more customers you will be able to attract. You will also be able to charge more for your service if you can offer that little bit extra.

Running a business from home

There are a number of advantages and disadvantages in running a business from your home. Legal restrictions, the effects on rates, insurance, tax and so on are dealt with in Chapter 3.

The pros
Start-up costs are low, and your income, relative to your outlay and hours of work, can be excellent (especially in comparison with other home workers). By working for yourself you'll gain a sense of accomplishment that you may not feel working for someone else. You can decide what hours you wish to work and you can fit your working hours around the care of children or other commitments that would make outside employment difficult. In addition, you save time and money that would be spent travelling to a workplace.

The cons
On the negative side you may be asked to work long hours or at unsocial times (eg evenings and weekends): customers often have

the impression that a home-based typing service works 24 hours a day (they would not expect this of an office-based typing agency). You might also find it difficult to integrate your work with your social life. When you work from home it is all too easy for family and friends to assume that your business is not very serious and to persist in interrupting you and/or expecting you to drop what you are doing in a way they wouldn't even consider if you were an employee or ran your business from separate premises. You will need to be very firm right from the start. Tell your family and friends what you are doing, explain what your working hours will be, and let them know that you will not appreciate interruptions during those hours. You will need to prevent yourself from falling into the same trap: it can be difficult to settle down to a typing assignment when the washing up is sitting in the sink!

Essential start-up equipment

The start-up equipment you need will depend on (a) where you will be doing your typing, (b) what kind of typing service you intend to offer, (c) how much time you want to invest in your business and (d) the income you require from it.

Your initial equipment will necessarily be geared to your aspirations of business success. While it would be rash to redecorate the spare-room, invest in a brand new office desk, filing cabinet, electronic typewriter and 20 reams of paper before you know there is an opening for your service, it would be equally unwise to start off with nothing but the family's battered manual typewriter and a few sheets of paper. In the latter case you may find yourself unnecessarily turning work away or discouraging potential customers with your lack of professionalism simply because you are not sufficiently equipped.

If you do start off with the minimum equipment in order to 'test the water' you should have a plan that will allow you to expand your business if it suddenly takes off. A typing service work-load can build up incredibly fast and the last thing you want when you're just starting out is to lose customers because you haven't enough paper to complete a job or because your typewriter ribbon has run dry.

The *bare minimum* necessary to start a typing service includes a typewriter (preferably electric or electronic), a desk or table (with drawers) on which to do the work, a ream of good quality ($85g/m^3$) A4 white typing paper and a small supply of envelopes, carbon paper, typewriter ribbons, pens, correction fluid (or ribbons), paper clips, and so on. You should also purchase the necessary bookkeeping stationery (see Chapter 4) *before* you start your business: you will very quickly get into a muddle if you don't and besides, you'll want to keep a record of the supplies you've already invested in the business to offset against your income later on.

Although it is not *absolutely* essential it is strongly recommended that you also have a telephone (connection costs about £95 + VAT in 1986), a dictionary, a diary (both to make appointments for customers and to keep track of your hours worked) and some means of protecting and storing customers' work (a small supply of manilla folders and a drawer to keep them in will suffice).

A more comprehensive checklist of initial supplies is included in Chapter 6, which will also help you to decide on the kind of equipment that best suits your needs and how to acquire it.

Start-up costs

Many families already own a typewriter, usually a portable manual model. And you will almost certainly have a table or a desk on which to use it. In this case (and assuming you are already on the phone and don't wish to invest much money to start with) you can start up your business for only a few pounds. Bear in mind, though, that electric and electronic typewriters are very popular now and produce a better quality finish than a manual. Your competitors may be using equipment that far outdates your own and *you* may lose custom as a result. In addition, portable typewriters usually have shorter carriages than office models and this may impose a restriction on the kind of work you can undertake. You will usually need a long carriage for typing accounts and certain legal documents, for example.

Hiring your typewriter can be a good idea because you can generally arrange for an immediate exchange if the machine breaks down, and hired typewriters usually come with a built-in maintenance agreement. If you prefer to buy, or can't hire in your area, you should consider a reconditioned second-hand model. These are generally much cheaper than new machines and are usually just as reliable, but make sure you get a guarantee. The price you pay can vary quite a lot: 1986 prices for *new* manual typewriters range from about £40 to £150, for electric typewriters from about £100 to £500, and for electronic models from about £150 to £600. The price variation is predominantly due to whether the model is compact or heavy duty and the range of features available. Expect to pay proportionately less for reconditioned models. If you are prepared to pay a few hundred pounds for an electric typewriter you should consider purchasing a word processor. These have fallen in price dramatically in recent years and some models can now be acquired (new) for under £500.

Other equipment can be bought second-hand. *Don't* buy a new desk and filing cabinet while you are working from home (unless you would have bought them for yourself anyway); wait until you are making sufficient profit to expand into a secretarial agency! You should be able to acquire a good quality second-hand desk, filing cabinet and all your start-up supplies for under £150. Again, how much you spend depends on how much you want, or need, to buy.

Initial start-up costs for a simple home-typing service can therefore range anywhere between £10 and £1000.

One major problem to beware of is being over-cautious initially. If you buy too cheaply to start with in order to avoid large losses in the event of your business failing, you risk losing money unnecessarily later on when you *have* to replace earlier purchases with more expensive equipment. Be realistic. If you intend to work full time at your business and hope to expand in the near future, then there is no point in buying a portable manual typewriter to start with. On the other hand, if you know from the outset that you will not be able to commit more than a few hours a week to the business and have no hope of expansion within the next five years or so, then it would be unwise to make expensive purchases of equipment initially – it will take you too long to recover the costs from your income. This is where forecasting and planning are essential. The next chapter will help you to formulate your business plans, an essential preliminary step. By the time you have done that you should be in a position to decide whether or not to leap into the ranks of the self-employed!

Chapter 2

Planning Your Strategy

Having a clear idea of the potential market for your service, how much you are going to charge for it, what your costs will be and how you will attract custom are crucial to any preparatory plan. Your aim, armed with the above knowledge, will be to provide a realistic forecast of the financial future of your venture. A well thought-out business plan will not only improve your chances of raising capital through your bank (if you need to) but will also provide a standard by which to measure the success of your typing service.

Many typing services are started up speculatively, without any preliminary research or financial plan: most of these are doomed to failure. Often the service is priced too low in the hope of attracting custom, and with relatively high initial costs the venture appears to be a failure. At this stage the service is often terminated on the assumption that the market is insufficient. A preliminary plan outlining initial and running costs, profit required (and therefore prices charged), the input of working hours necessary to achieve this, sensibly calculated, and an estimated period by which profits should have reached the required level will allow the success or otherwise of the venture to be much more realistically determined. Remember, a typing service needs time to build up custom.

Assessing the demand in your area

The first thing you must do is to find out what demand there is likely to be in your area. (A look at Chapter 5 will be helpful here.) To do this you will need to find the answers to several questions.

Are there any secretarial agencies or home-based typing services already operating in your area?

Most towns have at least one secretarial agency. These are often combined with printing/photocopying services, office supplies sales, computer services, 'temps' agencies and so on. Office-based agencies will need to charge quite a lot more than you because their overheads are much higher. Look them up in Yellow Pages then phone them and find out what their rates are (most charge by the hour) and how long it would take them to type, say, a 20,000-word dissertation. (This will give you some idea of the work-load they have.) Find out what is included in their charge. Do they include a copy? How much would they charge for extra copies? Is the work produced on a word processor or a typewriter? Will they charge extra if you want to make a few alterations later on?

Next, find out where the home-typing services are located. Home-typists usually advertise in the local press, in shop windows, on university bulletin boards and so on. If there are home-typists advertising regularly in your area you can be sure that there must be *some* demand for the kind of business you want to set up. Phone them up to find out their rates, how they charge, how fast their turnaround is etc. Don't pretend to be a potential customer – they will probably realise you're not genuine anyway – and besides, you may find useful contacts this way. Explain that you are thinking about setting up a home-based typing service of your own and are seeking advice from other home-typists. They may be able to give you first-hand advice about running such a business locally. If there are other home-typists near you perhaps you could arrange to pass on any 'overflow' to each other. Customers are more likely to try again if, rather than simply saying you can't fit in their work at that time, you can helpfully pass them on to another typist who is not so busy.

Are there any clubs, charities, small organisations or societies in your area?

The best places to find a list of local societies and organisations are your library and town hall. Most boroughs produce an annual list (usually free). Sometimes the list is kept in the library for reference only (you will need to take a pen and paper to make a note of likely addresses). Drama groups and writers' societies often need to have manuscripts typed and other organisations need typed agendas, minutes, accounts etc. If there are many small societies in your vicinity you may well be able to attract business from them.

What higher educational establishments are there in your area?

Don't restrict yourself to your own town or village on this one. If you are lucky enough to live near a college or university, go in and enquire about the possibility of typing dissertations. Typists advertise on the numerous notice boards in these establishments; however, many colleges keep a list of potential dissertation typists in their central office. If you want to break into this market you may be favoured if you can offer something special, such as correction of bad grammar/spelling/English, or a very fast turnaround. Students are notorious for wanting their dissertations typed up at the last minute!

Will you be able to attract small businesses that are lacking an inside secretarial staff and/or larger organisations with seasonal work overloads?

The answer to this question really depends on (a) where *you* are located relative to your potential customers, (b) whether you can attract trade with effective advertising (see Chapter 5) and (c) the extent of your own business training and office skills. Did you work for a local employer who might pass work on to you? In this area of the market more than any other you will be expected to be entirely businesslike, competent and trustworthy. You must be able to convince your clients that you can do a thoroughly professional job at a much more economical rate than an office-based secretarial agency.

If you want to enter this market you will probably need to consider whether you can offer any additional services which will attract customers, eg collection/delivery, on-site filing, telephone answering, photocopying, audio-typing, part-time work at your customer's premises, direct mailing and so on.

This is probably one of the most difficult markets to assess in advance. Sending out a mail shot to potential local business is probably the best way to probe this market. Advice on how to make the most of this approach is included in Chapter 5. You should be able to get a good idea of the number of small businesses in your vicinity from your Yellow Pages or your Thomson local directory; unfortunately, there is no way of knowing at this stage which of these might need outside secretarial help.

What opportunities are there for attracting business from the ordinary residents in your area?

This will depend on a wide variety of factors. The age structure, employment rate and size of population will give you an indication of the numbers of people who are likely to need assistance with the production of a CV, for example; you will not be asked to type many of these if you live in a small village of predominantly retired people.

25

Apart from CVs, application forms and a few letters, ordinary individuals rarely require the services of a typist, so this is not likely to be a very lucrative market on its own – you will probably need to attract business from other sources too.

Are there opportunities to offer a service through the mail?
Finally, don't think you have to restrict yourself totally to the area in which you live. Many people are quite happy to send non-urgent typing material through the post if they hold a duplicate copy. If you advertise a particular postal service – perhaps in a specialist journal – you may be able to generate business from people outside your own area. This is particularly true if you can offer something extra, such as translation-typing or a special knowledge of scientific terms (for contributors to a scientific journal for example). Take a close look at your own skills: an ability you take for granted may be just what another person is looking for.

What kind of typing will you do?

Having made a preliminary assessment of the potential market in your area you will need to consider whether your service can cater for any or all aspects of that market. What particular skills do you possess; are you confident of taking on any kind of typing assignment or do you wish to restrict your service to a particular field? In the initial stages, you would be well advised to take on *any* typing work you can get – not only will this give you practice in tackling work you have perhaps never come across before, it will also increase your knowledge of the market available, provide experience in dealing with different kinds of client and make more contacts for you. In this way you will find out not only what you prefer to do, but also which assignments are the most lucrative and offer the most consistent work-load.

Don't worry if you've never seen a properly laid out CV, a dissertation or the minutes of a meeting before – you must expect to learn as you go along. Your service will attract more custom and will be more successful the more broadly based it is.

Once you have acquired a good, regular, supply of customers you can begin to think about specialising. You will have an established business and plenty of experience to start from. If you choose to specialise you need to be especially sure of your market. Many specialist home-typists work for only one or two big clients (perhaps doing overflow typing, envelope addressing or invoices).

This can have advantages and disadvantages.

One home typist, although working in a self-employed capacity, did virtually all her work for one large client. Things went well for a few years, the work was easy, she was not troubled with dealing with new customers or chasing up debtors, and the supply of work was well regulated to suit her requirements. Unfortunately, when her client went out of business, so did she. Her client did not bother to inform her of the impending closure and she had no time to build up a supply of other customers to replace the lost income. Although this woman was not actually specialising in terms of the typing work she was equipped to do, the fact that she had limited her range of customers to such an extent had a similar effect.

You can specialise in terms of the kind of work you handle without necessarily restricting the number of clients you work for. If you can translate, index, summarise or understand technical jargon you may well be able to attract sufficient business from further afield to specialise in a particular type of work. However, unless you work primarily for a few established customers or your service is one that spreads by word of mouth, you may need to advertise almost continuously in trade journals or the press in order to generate enough business.

You might also like to consider related services such as bookkeeping, telephone answering and envelope addressing. This last occupation, however, has many pitfalls of which you should be aware. First and foremost *never respond to an advertisement which asks you to send money*. You don't pay people to address envelopes for them, *they* pay you. Second, don't be misled by firms that provide advertising postcards but want *you* to pay for posting them (usually on a commission for sales basis); you are very unlikely to make more in commission than you pay in postage. There are, of course, respectable firms who *do* use envelope addressers but these firms rarely need to advertise.

Try writing to companies in your area that do mass mailings: clubs, large retailers and organisations. Try the firms that send *you* advertisements through the post. Most of these pay a set, and rather low, rate for addressing a box of envelopes (which *they* provide). You should be paid more if you also fill, seal and stamp the envelopes.

How much time have you got?

Another factor you will need to consider is the amount of time you have available to devote to your service. For many small businesses the hours of work are relatively fixed – nobody wants their chimney swept at 10 pm or expects their local hairdressing salon to be open on Sunday afternoon – but this is not the case with a home-typing service. Unless you specify otherwise, you will find that many of your customers *will* expect you to work in the evenings and at weekends. There is no reason why you should, of course, although offering a fast-turnaround service is a good way of attracting custom, but remember that your earning potential will be limited by the number of hours you put into the business as well as your relative availability to customers (whether or not you are prepared to fit in an urgent piece of work even though this involves working unsocial hours).

Consider what hours you are prepared to work. Will these hours be fixed (say 9.00–5.00 four days a week) or do you want to work on a more flexible time-scale? Will you be restricted to working entirely from home or will you be able, and willing, to work outside your home base?

The amount you can earn from your business is obviously restricted by the number of hours you work. Once you have decided how much you want to earn per week, you can calculate the number of hours you need to work in order to achieve this goal. Bear in mind that some of your time will be spent interviewing customers, proof-reading, correcting mistakes, answering the telephone, maintaining records and so on. You must make an allowance for this 'non-typing' time when you estimate both the time required to complete a certain assignment and the rate you will charge. Make sure that your charges are sufficient to cover the number of hours you are putting into the business, not just those hours spent typing.

Your financial plan

By now you have made an assessment of the market for a typing service, considered your ability to enter that market and decided how much time you are going to devote to your business. You are now in a position to draw up your business plan. This is basically a financial forecast in which you will be attempting to foresee the likely profits generated by your service based on the time, charges, and expenses you estimate will be incurred.

Step 1. Decide how far ahead to plan. Although it may take some time for your typing service to start generating a good profit, you should not plan too far into the future. Make an assessment based on one year of business – you should really be making a good profit from your business well before the end of your first year since your initial expenses will be fairly low compared with other small businesses.

Step 2. Decide how much you expect to earn each month. To estimate this you will need to work out what your charges are going to be – Chapter 4 will help if you are unsure – and how much work you expect to generate. It is probably fairly realistic to assume that you will be working at your full capacity in six months' time. Estimate the progressive build-up of work in the preceding months.

Step 3. Calculate the costs involved in providing this level of service. This will include all your expenses – paper, ribbons, electricity used, telephone calls, insurance, interest on loans to purchase equipment, depreciation of equipment, advertising costs and so on.

Step 4. By taking the costs and expenses incurred from the total amount you expect to earn each month, you will be left with your net profit. (You may find that this projects as a net loss for the first month or so, especially if you intend to purchase a lot of expensive equipment and spend a relatively large amount on initial advertising.)

Assuming all goes according to plan, this is the profit you can expect to make on your typing service. From it you can decide whether your plan meets with your expectations, or whether you will need to modify it: for example, by increasing your charges. You will need to allow for the payment of National Insurance and income tax out of your net profit.

The following hypothetical financial plan for a home-typing service is intended to assist you in producing your own forecast.

Jane Doe left work to start a family. Now her children are at school she decides to start up a typing service from home. She converts part of her spare-bedroom into an office and, with her own savings, buys a word processor and printer for £400 and other equipment (second-hand desk, bookkeeping requisites, stapler, files, storage discs etc) for £100. She purchases a supply of typing paper, carbon paper, ribbons and so forth. These are consumed as part of the service and are grouped under 'expenses'. She starts business in January. Depreciation on her resaleable equipment is estimated at £5 per month (see Chapter 4).

Jane expects to earn £3.00 per hour (her charges will be slightly higher than this to allow for time spent interviewing, proof-reading and so on) and, assuming she achieves a full work-load by June, her service will be bringing in £420 per month. (She intends to work seven hours a day, 20 days per month.)

She estimates her total expenses for the year: advertising, printing business cards, telephone, postage, insurance, electricity, repairs and maintenance, direct costs (paper, envelopes, ribbons etc) and so forth and then divides this by 12 to get a monthly figure. If she was doing seasonal work she should allocate income and expenses more realistically to the relevant months.

From her financial plan it is clear that Jane Doe's typing service is likely to be a success in the long term. But this plan is rather simplistic. First, costs incurred have been spread out over the whole year. In fact, most of the expenses would be concentrated in the first few months, especially advertising, ensuring adequate stocks of paper and so on were available, printing of business cards etc. If you want a more realistic month-by-month idea of cash flow, you will need to estimate the *actual* amount spent/earned each month. Even so, according to this forecast Jane does not make any real profit until March. Had costs been distributed more realistically, she may have expected to run at a loss for three months or more.

Had Jane Doe not made a financial forecast, she might well have dissolved Typing Galore after three or four months because her business appeared to be a failure. By preparing a financial plan she can see not only the future potential of her service, but also whether or not her *actual* business is following the expected trend, and hence whether her original estimates were accurate or need revision.

Going it alone or in partnership?

The Jane Doe example given above is based on one type of business structure – that of the *sole trader*. The majority of home-typing services start off on this basis and it is the simplest form of business management. If you wish to operate as a sole trader and intend to run the service under your own name there are no legal formalities – you simply inform the Inland Revenue and the Department of Health and Social Security that you have begun trading. (See Chapter 3 if you intend to use a business name.) One of the disadvantages of sole trading is that there is no distinction in law between the owner and the business. The debts and obligations of the business are regarded as those of the owner.

Financial Plan – Jane Doe trading as Typing Galore

	J	F	M	A	M	J	J	A	S	O	N	D
Income	50	100	180	260	360	420	420	420	420	420	420	420
Expenses	70	70	70	70	70	70	70	70	70	70	70	70
Depreciation	5	5	5	5	5	5	5	5	5	5	5	5
Profit (Loss)												
– per month	(25)	25	105	185	285	345	345	345	345	345	345	345
– cumulative	(25)	—	105	290	575	920	1265	1610	1955	2300	2645	2990

Consequently, creditors may make claims on your personal estate for any debts owed to them by your business. On the other hand, because owner and business are one, any profit made belongs to the proprietor and is subject to income tax. Another possible disadvantage of sole trading is that you lack the support of colleagues (and their help), and need to have expertise in a number of areas if your business is to be successful.

On the other hand, you may know one or more other people who are interested in starting up a typing service. By pooling capital, labour and expertise you may be able to operate a more successful business than if you opted to go it alone. A *partnership* can be started without any legal formalities if trading under the surnames of all the partners (though again the DHSS and Inland Revenue must be informed), and can comprise any number of proprietors from two to 20.

Although it is not a legal necessity it is advisable to have a formal agreement between the partners drawn up by a solicitor. If you don't do this the provisions of the Partnership Act 1890 will apply. (The legal position of a partnership is different in Scotland from that in the rest of the UK.) See also Chapter 10, page 130, on partnerships.

As for sole traders, partners are responsible for the debts incurred by the business and all are entitled to a share of the profits. One important point worth emphasising is that *all* partners are responsible for the debts of the business. This means that if your partner makes a rash purchase and then disappears, the suppliers can turn to you for payment. The same applies to income tax. If your partner fails to pay income tax on his share of the profits the Inland Revenue can ask *you* to pay it.

Great care should be exercised in the choice of partners. Many partnerships go wrong because disputes and disagreements occur which had not been foreseen – going into partnership with someone can ruin a perfectly good friendship. Pick partners who you are sure are committed and responsible. If they have skills and abilities which complement your own you will both benefit more from the partnership than if you pick someone with similar abilities. Partnerships *can* work, but they are often very problematical.

The principal disadvantage of the sole trader or the partnership lies in the fact that the owner(s) carry an unlimited liability for the debts and obligations of the business. This can be overcome by forming a private limited liability company. Typing services do not usually operate in this way, though it may be worth considering when your business reaches the stage of expansion into a secretarial bureau. The limited company is bound by much stricter legal requirements and constraints than a sole trader or partnership and is more suitable for ventures where the risk of financial loss is relatively high. Since most creditors including banks, especially in the early days of a venture, will require personal guarantees for the amount of credit or loan, you may not be any more protected by forming a limited company than you would be operating as a sole trader or partnership.

Chapter 3

Starting Your Business

For many people the actual setting up of their business seems to be the most difficult stage in the whole operation. Don't be put off by the necessary, but sometimes rather daunting, red tape involved. The legal requirements are really very simple (assuming you have elected to operate as a sole trader or partnership) and you should have little difficulty if you follow the advice given here.

Legal requirements – people you need to inform

Anyone can start up a business, trading under their own name without any legal formalities whatsoever. You can employ staff and buy or lease property and equipment in connection with the business.

However many hours you work in your business and whether or not you are also in paid employment you must inform your local Inspector of Taxes within a few days of commencing your service. His address appears in the local telephone directory under 'Inland Revenue'. You will probably be asked to complete form 41G which asks for basic particulars of yourself, your business and your previous employment. If you have given up paid employment to start up your typing service your local Inspector of Taxes may also require your P45 (a form detailing your income and tax paid which should be given to you by your employer when you leave).

You should also inform the local office of the Department of Health and Social Security. Do this *before* you actually start your service otherwise you could lose any entitlement you may have to be exempted from paying National Insurance contributions (see Chapter 4).

Your home

Rates and planning permission
Although the General Rate Act 1967 says that only premises 'used

wholly for the purpose of a private dwelling-house' attract the domestic rate, you should not have to pay higher rates if you use a room for business typing. The rating authorities consider the nature and extent of the business in determining whether additional charges must be made. If you convert your front room into a secretarial agency and erect a large sign outside your rates may well be increased (and you would also require planning permission for such an extensive change of use). However, if you make only minor alterations to your premises – for example converting part of a spare-room into an office – you are not obliged to inform the rates department nor obtain planning permission, and your rates should not be affected.

If you rent rather than own your home, check the terms of your tenancy agreement. Although most tenancy agreements preclude the use of the premises for business purposes, they do not normally forbid the operation of a small part-time business such as a typing service, provided that it does not disturb other tenants. It is probably wise to inform your landlord that you intend to do occasional typing work from home and ask for his confirmation that this is in order. He may look on this more favourably than if he finds out through the grapevine that you are carrying on a small business from his premises without his knowledge!

It is wise to check the deeds if you own your house or flat, because they may contain a covenant specifically excluding business use.

Capital gains tax

The advantage of setting aside part of your home primarily for the use of your typing service is that you can claim a proportion of heating/lighting and so on for tax relief under Schedule D. The drawback is that the Inland Revenue may levy capital gains tax on the proportion of the profit from the sale equal to the proportion of the premises used for your work. However, the tax is only payable if there is *exclusive* business use of the room(s). You can avoid it by ensuring that your office is also used for domestic purposes from time to time, as a spare bedroom for guests, maybe, or a place for the children to do their homework.

Neighbours

Neighbours are another potential problem depending on the district in which you live and the type of premises you occupy. Consider carefully whether your typing service will cause any inconvenience or annoyance to them. If you expect most of your clients to visit you, are you sure there is sufficient room for them to park their cars for short periods without causing an obstruction? Will clients have to use a shared access to reach your premises? Will the noise of your typing disturb anyone? (This is especially relevant to people living in flats, or if you intend to work late into the evening.) The best way of avoiding problems is to inform your immediate neighbours in advance of your intentions, and take a reasonable attitude to any complaints raised. You should be able to reduce any problems caused by noise by sensible location of your office, and the use of mats and covers or 'quiet' machines. If parking or access is likely to be a problem you can either ask that your clients visit only during certain hours (for example, when you know your neighbours are likely to be out) or ensure that they park their cars at an appropriate place.

Choosing and using a business name

Although the majority of home-typing services operate under the name of the owner, there are advantages to be had from using a business name. Your advertising may have more impact and people may remember your service better if you have a catchy business name – hence you may generate more business than you would if you operated under your own name. Also, the use of a business name may add an element of professionalism to your service which may also attract more custom. Finally, if your service is a great success and you eventually want to expand into a secretarial agency you can take your (already well known) business name with you and so ensure that your established customers know where you have gone.

The Companies Act 1981 repealed the Registration of Business Names Act 1916 so it is no longer necessary for business names to be registered. There are, however, restrictions on permissible names and a requirement to comply with the regulations of the new act. You cannot, for example, use the same business name as another in the same field or a confusingly similar name, and your business name must not give the impression that it is connected with Her Majesty's government or any local authority. The best way to ensure you are complying with this is to look up the typing services and agencies operating in your area and make sure you are not using one of their business names (or a very similar one). Also, make sure you don't use the name of any well-known secretarial agencies despite the fact that it might be your name too – even if they don't have a branch in your area. (It is possible that you will choose a name that is being used by another small typing service elsewhere in the country; however, it is very unlikely to seek an injunction against you for misleading people into thinking your business is the same.)

To comply with the terms of the Companies Act 1981 the owners of a business must:

- state their names and addresses on all business stationery;
- display in a prominent place on the business premises a notice containing their names and addresses; and
- give their names and addresses in writing to any business contact who asks for that information.

These regulations should not cause any significant problems unless you intend to swindle your customers! You should simply include your name and address and those of your partner(s) on your business stationery, business cards, invoices and so on. You don't need to divulge this information in an advertisement although you will probably want to include at least your telephone number and probably also your address. The regulation about displaying a business name on your premises is not really intended for a business run from the owner's home (since it's relatively easy for your clients to find out who you are, and they already know where you live) but you can put up a notice in your 'office', or wherever you normally interview your clients, stating the name of your business together with your name and address.

So the legal requirements are fairly straightforward. Actually *choosing* a suitable business name is not necessarily so easy. Ideally, you should chose a name that not only 'sounds' like a typing service (or the particular variation you have in mind), but is also easy to remember and conveys an idea of the kind of service you are operating. You can use real words – for example, 'Typing Galore' – or make up new words that sound appropriate – for example, 'Wizzword'. Try to think of a name that gives the right impression of your particular service. Perhaps you are offering a very high quality business service with a guarantee of accuracy. You will want to convey the sense of quality, service and accuracy in your business name – something like 'Top Flight Typing' or 'Executype' might be appropriate. If you are offering a fast-turnaround word-processing service you will want to emphasise other aspects – perhaps 'Wizzword' would be appropriate here, or 'Fast Fingers'. If you are totally stuck it might help to write down all the features of your service that you feel are important or special. Next list all the words you can think of that relate to those features and then try combinations of those words and part words. You should come up with several 'catchy' sounding names. Now all you need to do is decide which one you are going to use for your typing service.

Bookkeeping

However small your typing service you should keep full and accurate records of all your takings and expenditures in relation to the business right from the start. Not only will the Inspector of Taxes require an accurate statement of your profits (he is entitled to estimate your profits if you cannot supply an accurate record) but you will soon lose track of the progress of your business, and may also have difficulty in chasing up non-paying clients or tracing purchases if you do not maintain a sensible record system. The subject is dealt with in greater detail in Chapter 4.

Insurance

Even while you are working from home you will need to have adequate insurance to cover not only loss or damage to your business equipment or large amounts of stock, but also to cover yourself against claims by your customers (public liability insurance) or any employees (employer's liability) as well as personal insurance for yourself. Your normal household contents policy should be sufficient to protect you against the loss of inexpensive items such as your pocket calculator but you may need to make special arrangements for more valuable items such as a typewriter, photocopier, telephone answering machine, mobile phone, and so on. Second, you should check the terms of your household contents policy carefully. Such policies are devised for private dwellings – if you are regularly visited by clients you may be required to pay a higher premium. If in doubt write to your insurance company informing them that you will be running a small typing service from your home and asking them to confirm whether or not this will affect your contents policy. Unless you plan to purchase a lot of expensive equipment and convert half your house into a typing bureau, you will probably find that your general contents insurance premium will not be increased.

If you are using your car extensively for business purposes (perhaps by operating a mobile secretarial service or a collection/delivery service) you will also need to ensure that your car insurance policy will cover you while you are officially working. Insurance is a complicated business and you would be well advised to consult an insurance broker, whose services are free of charge to clients (they receive a commission from insurance companies).

Your insurance broker will tell you what insurance is necessary for your particular requirements and will shop around for the best deal for you. Most reputable brokers are members of the British Insurance Brokers' Association.

Help and advice for new businesses

Perhaps the first sources people think of when seeking advice on setting up a new business are the bank manager, solicitor and accountant. The advice of your bank manager will probably be free but you will normally have to pay for advice from your solicitor and accountant. Unless you are starting up a fairly extensive home-typing service – say a partnership, or with a small staff – you are not likely to need the professional advice of a solicitor or accountant at this stage although you may need to consult your bank manager if you wish to borrow money to buy equipment.

A number of organisations now specialise in offering advice and information to small businesses. The Small Firms Service, which is run by the Department of Employment provides a nationwide counselling service to owners of small businesses, including home-based typing services and has 12 regional centres in England. In Scotland the Small Firms Service is operated through the Scottish Development Agency and in Wales through the Welsh Development Agency. A similar service is provided in Northern Ireland through the Department of Economic Development.

The Small Firms Service can be contacted most easily by telephone: dial 100 and ask the operator for Freefone Enterprise. You will be put in touch with a professional business counsellor in your district who will be able to offer free advice on all aspects of setting up and running a small business. Alternatively you can write to the Small Firms Division of the Department of Employment. As well as direct consultations, the Small Firms Service also produces a range of free leaflets which provides useful general information on setting up a business, basic bookkeeping, marketing, employing staff and so on.

If you live in an English rural area the Council for Small Industries in Rural Areas (CoSIRA) offers a similar service.

CoSIRA's headquarters are at 141 Castle Street, Salisbury, Wiltshire SP1 3TP (tel: 0722 336255); they can put you in touch with your nearest CoSIRA centre. In rural Wales a similar service is offered by the Development Board for Rural Wales and in Scotland by the Highlands and Islands Development Board and the Scottish Development Agency.

In addition there are now numerous local enterprise agencies which offer free advice and information to small businesses in the area. These agencies are usually founded by an association of local industry, commerce, educational establishment and the public sector, to assist and encourage local economic growth. You can find out if there is one near you by contacting Business in the Community.

Chapter 4
Finance and Accounting

Raising money

Assuming you start up your typing service using your own home as a base, you should not require a great deal of capital to purchase the necessary equipment. Later on, when your business has grown and you wish to move into separate premises and acquire more equipment, you will possibly need to raise more finance.

The cheapest way to finance your typing service is to use your own money – personal savings, redundancy money, saleable assets (jewellery/antiques) and so forth. If you do not have sufficient personal funds there are several ways in which you can raise money to purchase your initial equipment.

Loans
A loan is perhaps the most obvious way to raising money. You may have friends or relatives who will either lend you money directly or guarantee a bank overdraft, or loan, on your behalf. Your bank will probably be willing to provide you with either an overdraft facility for several months or a direct loan – especially if you are an established customer – but they will want to see a business plan showing your setting-up costs, expected income, fixed and variable costs, and overheads. The advantage of an overdraft is that interest (usually two to three per cent above base lending rate) is only paid on the actual amount by which you are overdrawn; the disadvantage is that it can be called in at any time. Overdrafts are usually agreed for only one year, with a review thereafter, whereas loans are more generally for two to five years. You can claim tax relief on bank charges and loan interest related to your typing service. There are also numerous private finance agencies who may well be prepared to give you a loan but their interest rates are often very high. If you are considering using a private financier consult your solicitor.

Hire purchase and leasing
Most office equipment can be acquired by either hire purchase or

leasing and this is often a good alternative to taking out a loan to purchase outright. If you are considering equipment on hire purchase check how much you will be paying over and above the direct sales price, and that the equipment eventually becomes your property. You may be able to get a better deal (pay less interest) by getting a loan and buying outright. Leasing equipment is a very good idea for a typing service. If you lease your typewriter, word processor, photocopier etc, you will pay a monthly rental and the equipment remains the property of the lessor. The major disadvantage of this is that you never ultimately own the equipment and can neither sell it nor use it as collateral for any other type of borrowing. On the other hand, you will normally be provided with an inbuilt maintenance agreement, a facility for rapid replacement if your machine breaks down and the ability to upgrade your equipment as and when necessary.

Enterprise Allowance Scheme

The Enterprise Allowance Scheme, set up by the government, is designed for those receiving unemployment benefit who would otherwise lose this income when they started up their own business. Details of the scheme can be obtained from Jobcentres but basically it provides successful applicants with £40 per week for a year to offset the loss of unemployment benefit and give their business time to 'get off the ground'. Any kind of business venture can apply, including home-based typing services. To qualify you must be over 18 but under retirement age, you must have been receiving unemployment benefit (or under a notice of redundancy) for at least eight weeks and you must show that you are prepared to invest at least £1000 in your business (this does not have to be in cash; you might already have equipment or a bank overdraft facility to this amount, for example). There is considerable demand for the scheme and you may have to wait some time to set up your business. You must not start your typing service before your application has been approved. Further information can be obtained from Jobcentres or by dialling 100 and asking for Freefone Enterprise.

A business bank account

You should seriously consider opening a separate bank account solely for your typing service as soon as you start operating your business. Although it is possible to use your own personal bank account (and you will almost certainly need some kind of bank account as many customers will want to pay by cheque), keeping track of the monies entering and leaving the account which are related to your service can become quite a headache. If your typing service is very small and your income from it very low, you should have few problems in using your personal bank account, If, however, you hope to expand your business in the future and/or receive a good income from it, then you should open a separate bank account when you start up.

Apart from making it easier for you to keep track of your typing profits, having a separate business bank account will also be an advantage if you need to dispute any tax assessments imposed by the Inland Revenue. It is obviously much easier for you to prove your income and outgoings if your service has its own bank account than if you have to attempt to separate your typing service banking from your personal banking.

Keeping records

While you are operating your typing service from home, you will probably not require the full range of accounts books normally used by businesses, although you will need to acquire these if your business expands. You can purchase various types of account books at stationery shops. If you are operating as a sole trader, do not employ staff, operate a system whereby you pay for purchases such as paper stocks immediately and your clients pay for their typing on delivery, you should be able to manage reasonably well with a simple cash-book system.

If you have a business bank account you may prefer to have two cash books, one for recording cash receipts and their payment into the bank and all withdrawals by cheque, standing order or direct debits and the other for recording payments into or out of the float of loose cash kept at your office. If you supply typing and invoice your customers for payment at a later date and/or you yourself similarly obtain goods or services on credit for the running of your business you will need to have separate books (called sales and purchases day books) for recording the amounts owing to you (debtors) and the amounts owed by you (creditors). You will need these figures not only for your own information but also for the preparation of your final accounts. In addition to your basic account book(s) you should have some means of securing or filing copies of invoices generated by yourself and receipts for purchases made in connection with the business. A filing cabinet is ideal but two large ring binder files will work just as well initially.

Bookkeeping is a chore to most small businesses, but it has to be done. Although it is absolutely essential to keep proper and accurate records right from the start, it really isn't very difficult. If you are absolutely hopeless at figures then you should consider hiring a bookkeeper to set up your records system and maintain interim checks that all is well. Many accountants and bookkeepers are self-employed and work from home (just like yourself). You should find a good selection in the Business Services section of your local newspaper, *and* their rates will be more reasonable than those of a large agency or group of accountants. You can also get a useful free leaflet from the Small Firms Service entitled 'Elements of Bookkeeping' by L A Rich and T J Terry.

You need to keep sensible and accurate records for two reasons. First, you will need records from which to extract your annual accounts to make assessments of your profits for VAT, National Insurance and tax purposes. Second, your records will provide valuable information *to you* on the performance of your typing service, allowing you to see where purchasing or costing policies need to be reviewed and efficiency improved.

The cash book

This is your most essential book (and perhaps the only one you will need initially). You can purchase a good quality cash book from any stationer or office supplier. It should have columns in which to insert the following (minimum) information: date, details of the receipt/payment, amount received/paid, and a column for inserting any folio/reference of your own, for example the invoice/receipt number or purchase number; this will allow you to locate the separately filed receipts, invoices and vouchers referred to in the cash book.

In your cash book you will record your receipts on the left-hand side of a double page spread and any payments you make on the right (see figure opposite). You can use the same book for both cash and cheque receipts and payments. You should keep your cash book up to date every day and it's a good idea to start a new double page every month and total up your receipts and payments at the end of every month. Your first entries will almost certainly be all on the 'payments' side; don't forget to include the purchase of your cash book as a payment!

Debtors

If you provide typing on credit terms for a few customers you can easily keep track of outstanding accounts by filing unpaid copy

RECEIPTS				PAYMENTS			
Date	Detail	Ref	Amount	Date	Detail	Ref	Amount
1986	Brought forward		402·00	1986	Brought forward		130·16
3/2	A. SMITH	102	40·00	4/2	PRINTERS LTD	26	14·28
5/2	B. JONES	103	13·50	10/2	STATIONERS LTD	27	36·12
6/2	S.W. LITTLE	104	24·00	21/2	POST OFFICE	28	10·50
12/2	M. BOOTH	105	58·60				
15/2	J.R. CLIFFE	106	2·50				
20/2	L. GRANGE	107	104·60				

Sample Cash Book

invoices in a ring binder. Check these every week to make sure your customers are not taking too long to pay you – you may need to send out reminders. When your customers pay you, bank the money, enter the receipt in the cash book and place the invoice in the file of paid invoices.

Creditors

As with sales invoices, if you have only a few purchase invoices each month, files for unpaid bills and paid bills will work reasonably well. When you actually pay the bill write it on the payments side of your cash book and move the invoice from the unpaid file to the other.

Sales and purchase day books and ledgers

If you purchase a large number of sales invoices (most of your customers pay you at a later date) and/or regularly defer payments, you may eventually need a sales day book in which to keep a record of invoices issued, when and to whom, and a purchase day book giving details of your supplier and the amount(s) owed.

The ledger sets out details, taken from sales and purchase day books, of individual customers' and suppliers' accounts and serves as a record of amounts owed and owing.

Although it is unlikely that you will need to extend your system much beyond the cash book stage if you are working as a sole trader from your home, you will almost certainly require sales and purchases journals and ledger if your service is more extensive or expands into a bureau.

Value added tax

There is a section detailing the options and requirements of being registered for VAT on page 53. It is very unlikely that your taxable turnover will be above the *compulsory* registration level while you are a sole trader, but if so you will have to keep *separate* records of the VAT you pay and the VAT you charge to your customers. This is not as complicated as is generally believed, especially if you keep your records up to date on a daily basis. You will either need to keep separate books to show VAT paid and received or have additional columns in your cash books (and journals) in which to separate VAT from the total receipts and payments.

Employees

If you employ staff then you will need to keep records of their pay, tax, and National Insurance for which you will need a wages book. You will be responsible for deducting tax from your employees' pay at source under the PAYE system – your local tax office will provide the necessary forms and advise you how to do this – and you will also be required to pay both the employer's and your employees' Class 1 National Insurance contributions (though you do, of course, deduct the employees' contributions from their earnings). Hence, if you have employees you will need to keep additional records that will enable you to keep track of your payments to them, and those made on their behalf (see page 47).

Annual accounts

The Inspector of Taxes will require you to prepare accounts each year in order to make an assessment of your taxable profit. You are not obliged to engage an accountant to prepare your accounts and, while you are still working from home, accounts prepared by yourself (so long as they meet with certain conventions and requirements) should be just as acceptable to the Inland Revenue as any that could be produced by an accountant. Having said that if, after reading this section, you are at all unsure about the presentation and layout of accounts, you should consider engaging an accountant to prepare your annual accounts for you. If you intend to do this you should make doubly sure that your daily records are adequate – this will help to reduce the fee that you have to pay your accountant. Bear in mind that many bookkeepers are able to produce accounts – a self-employed bookkeeper may be

Name	NI No.	Contribution Table Letter	Gross Amount Due	Employers Deductions			Net Amount Due	Employers Contributions	
				Tax	Class 1			Class 1	
R. SMITH	7K02,198	A	636·07	129·60	55·65		450·82	77·59	

Sample Wages Book

47

able to prepare your accounts at a fraction of the fee charged by a firm of accountants.

If you engage an accountant the Inspector of Taxes will normally deal directly with him rather than with you. Tax returns and formal notices of assessment of tax, however, will be sent direct to you.

The date to which you make up your accounts is entirely for you to decide. Form 41G (from the Inland Revenue) requires you to specify your proposed accounting date, so you will probably decide this when you start your business. Pick a date that will be convenient for you – perhaps the end of your first year of trading, or the calender year end, 31 December, or even the end of the tax year, 5 April. Once you have chosen your accounting date you should make up your accounts to that date each year and submit them to your local Inspector of Taxes.

The accounts you supply to the Inspector are usually in two parts: the profit and loss account (which summarises the year's transactions) and the balance sheet (which shows the assets and liabilities of your typing service at the chosen accounting date).

Preparing your profit and loss account

Your profit and loss account will show your gross profit, or how much money you have actually received, on the right-hand side and your expenses, usually broken down into sections, on the left-hand side. Your net profit (or loss) is then shown as the difference between these two figures. The following example should make these points clearer:

Profit and Loss Account of Susan Smith Trading as Typewise Typing Service for the year ended 31 December 19--

		£	£
Gross income from work done			5,500.86
Less:	Depreciation	58.00	
	Advertising	350.85	
	Stationery & Supplies	460.98	
	Printing (business cards)	25.00	
	Postage	23.35	
	Telephone	4.60	
	Electricity	35.60	980.38
Net Profit			4,520.48

In assessing the expenses for heating and lighting used in relation to your business, it is conventional to apportion your *actual* electricity/gas bill on the basis of the proportion of your home used primarily for running your typing service. If you have a six-roomed house and use one room primarily for your service for example, you could claim up to one-sixth of your heating/lighting bill as a business expense. It is probably better if you try to maintain an accurate record of the number and times of telephone calls you make in connection with your business – you can claim the cost of these as a business expense.

Remember to include *all* your expenses. If you use your car (for example, to collect and deliver work), then you should claim for the petrol used. If you have to pay an additional premium on your house insurance because you work from home, include this as an expense. You should also include any wages paid to your employees, interest on business loans or overdrafts, any professional fees you pay, and depreciation.

You *cannot* claim your National Insurance contributions (or income tax) as an 'expense', nor should you include any solely personal or domestic expenses.

Preparing your balance sheet
Your balance sheet is a record of the money (capital) you have invested in the business, the value of your fixed assets (typewriter) and current assets (balance at bank), and any liabilities you have (loan, creditors). An example is shown below:

Balance Sheet of Susan Smith
(trading as Typewise Typing Service)
as at 31 December 19--

	£	£
Fixed Assets		
Typewriter	500.00	
less depreciation	50.00	450.00
Desk	80.00	
less depreciation	8.00	72.00
Current Assets		
Sundry Debtors		102.85
Balance at Bank		450.00
TOTAL ASSETS		1,074.85

Capital		480.85
add Net Profit for year	4,520.48	
less Drawings	4,070.48	450.00
Sundry Creditors		144.00
TOTAL LIABILITIES		1,074.85

Your balance sheet shows the state of affairs on a particular date.

Depreciation is an estimate of the reduction in value of your fixed assets (excluding premises, which usually increase in value) over the year. There are several methods of estimating depreciation, the commonest being the 'straight line method'. By this method you estimate the useful life of the asset and its residual value (how much it will be worth) at the end of that time, then divide the amount to be written off by the end of the estimated life giving a fixed amount of depreciation each year.

Example

A word processor is purchased for	£450
Residual value estimated at	£ 70
Leaving (to be written off)	£380

Estimated life – 7 years
Annual depreciation = £380/7 = £54

Capital and Revenue. An important convention is the separation of 'capital' and 'revenue' expenditure. Revenue expenditure is the day-to-day running costs of the service and is included in your profit and loss account whereas capital expenditure is of a more permanent nature with which 'assets' are purchased (eg a new typewriter) and this is shown in your balance sheet and is *not* debited as an expense in your profit and loss account. It is not always easy to make the distinction. Clearly a typewriter is a capital item and the cost of repairs to it is revenue expenditure, but what about a new carriage and platen? Usually common sense is the best guide in making such distinctions. Note, however, that capital expenditure is eventually paid for out of revenue: the typewriter is written off in the profit and loss account.

Income tax

Everyone is entitled to earn some money without paying tax on it.

For a married couple (whether or not the wife is working) this is £3655 per annum and for single people and married women the allowance is £2335 per annum (1986–87). For those over retirement age the allowance is £2850 for a single person and £4504 for a married couple.

In other words if you are a married woman then £2335 is the amount you can earn (your net profit) before you are liable to pay income tax. Assuming you do not have any other income, then you will have to pay tax on any profit you make in excess of £2335. If you are also in employment and pay tax through a PAYE scheme, then you will probably be liable to pay income tax on the *whole* of your typing service profit because your personal allowance will have been taken into account in your employment. Unless you apply to be taxed separately from your husband (this may be financially beneficial if your combined income is relatively high) your income will normally be included on his tax return.

Tax on the profits of your typing service will usually be paid in two equal instalments on 1 January and 1 July. Some time after you send in your annual accounts the Inspector of Taxes will send you a notice of assessment telling you how much tax you will be required to pay and when.

At present there is a sliding scale of tax levied on income above the relevant personal allowance, starting at 29 per cent. Unless you are making more than £17,201 per annum you will not be liable for any higher taxation than this. Returning to the example given earlier, Susan Smith's profit and loss account showed her net profit for the year to be £4520.48. Her tax assessment would therefore be:

Net income	£4,520.48
Less personal allowance	£2,335.00
Taxable income	£2,185.48

Tax payable £2,185.48 @ 29% = £633.78
in two instalments of £316.89

If your profits are likely to exceed your personal allowance you should take care to put money aside for tax later on. You may be charged interest on overdue tax so it is in your best interests to have the money available for payment at the appropriate times. If you are in doubt your local tax office should be able to advise you. Details of the basis of tax assessment, among other things, are also included in a free booklet issued by the Inland Revenue entitled 'Starting in Business'.

National Insurance

There are four classes of National Insurance contribution. Briefly, these are:

Class 1.   Paid by people who work for an employer (subject to various conditions not covered here).

Class 2.   Paid by *self-employed* people (see below for conditions).

Class 3.   Voluntary contributions for people not liable for either Class 1 or Class 2 contributions.

Class 4.   'Earnings-related' contributions for *self-employed* people who have profits between certain limits.

If you are employed and wish to run your typing service in your spare time you may be liable for both Class 1 *and* Class 2 (and possibly Class 4) contributions. Your employer will arrange for the payment of your Class 1 contributions and you must arrange for the payment of any other contributions. If you are not employed then you may be liable to pay Class 2 and possibly also Class 4 contributions, depending on how much profit you make.

Class 2 contributions are paid weekly either by direct debit from your bank account or by stamping a contribution card, which the DHSS will send you on request, with stamps bought weekly from a post office. The current (1986–87) rate of Class 2 contribution is £3.75 per week. Class 4 contributions are earnings-related and are normally calculated, assessed and collected by the Inland Revenue at the same time as income tax on your business profits. Leaflet IR24 (Inland Revenue) explains how profits are assessed for Class 4 contributions and leaflets NI41 and NP18 give details of the rates of Class 4 contributions and the age limits of contributors.

You will be *exempt* from paying National Insurance contributions if:

1.   you are over retirement age or under 16, or
2.   you are entitled to reduced contribution liability as a married woman or widow (you must have exercised your option not to pay Class 2 contributions before 11 May 1977), or
3.   your earnings from your typing service are below the small-earnings limit (£2025 per annum in 1986–87).

In order to be exempt from Class 2 contributions you must apply for a 'Certificate of Exception' from your local DHSS office (ask for leaflets NI27A and CF11).

Normally, your profits from the previous year are used in the assessment of your eligibility for exception from Class 2 payments. However, if in your first year of trading, you expect to make less than the small-earnings limit, you can still apply for exception. Your DHSS will expect you to provide evidence to support your claim so you will have to show that you have made a reasonable estimate of your likely earnings. In subsequent years they will require a copy of your annual accounts if you wish to have your exception certificate extended.

Although it is a good idea to avoid paying National Insurance contributions unnecessarily, especially if your business is very small or takes a long time to build up, your entitlement to the benefits afforded by National Insurance may be affected. If you are concerned about your entitlement to any National Insurance benefits (pensions, sickness benefit, maternity allowance etc) you should ask your local DHSS office for advice before you decide to apply for exception. You can get advice by telephone by dialling 100 and asking for Freefone DHSS.

Value added tax

Compulsory registration
If your taxable turnover, that is the amount of money your service earns per annum rather than your net profit, exceeds a certain amount (£20,500 in 1986–87) you must register with your local VAT office (you can find them in the telephone directory under HM Customs and Excise) and charge VAT at 15 per cent to your customers. This tax is paid by you to Customs and Excise. It is highly unlikely that your business will reach this level of turnover while you are working single-handed from home, though you should keep an eye on your income and notify the VAT office if your turnover exceeds £7000 (1986–87) in any quarter.

Voluntary registration
You can apply for *voluntary* registration if your taxable turnover is below the compulsory registration limits, but you will have to satisfy Customs and Excise that you have a 'compelling and continuous business need for registration' (HM Customs and Excise Notice 700/1/86).

Advantages of being registered

The advantage of being registered is that you can offset the VAT you will have to pay for supplies and equipment against the VAT you will be able to charge your customers. If you receive more VAT than you pay, the difference has to be paid to Customs and Excise. If you pay more VAT than you receive you can reclaim the difference.

Disadvantages of being registered

The disadvantages are (a) your customers will have to pay more than they would if you weren't registered and you may lose custom as a result; (b) you will have to keep accurate and separate records of all VAT paid and charged, as well as completing a VAT return every three months and having visits by VAT officers; (c) you will normally have to remain registered for two years from the date of issue of your VAT registration certificate (even if your registration was voluntary) and (d) the regulations governing what is 'standard rated' and what is 'zero rated' or 'exempt' is rather complex. You would have to charge VAT at 15 per cent on an individual letter, for example, but if you typed up an A4 leaflet and provided 50 copies of it VAT would be 0 per cent (zero rated).

Further advice about VAT

If you think you might need to (or prefer to) register for VAT you should get advice from your local VAT office who can also provide several free leaflets among which 'Should I Be Registered for VAT?' (700/1/86), 'The Ins and Outs of VAT' (700/15/84), 'Printed and Similar Matter' (701/21/86) and 'Keeping Records and Accounts' (700/21/86) are particularly useful.

Changes in income tax, National Insurance and VAT

The figures quoted above are correct at the time of going to press (1986–87). However, personal allowances, NI contribution rates, lower earnings limits and VAT registration limits among other things, are reviewed annually, and announced in the Budget. You should check the current rates with the appropriate authorities.

Pensions

It may seem a bit pre-emptive to ask you to consider your pension (state or personal) at this stage but it is a matter to which you should give some thought if you are seriously intent on becoming self-employed.

How much you will get from the *state* when you retire depends on the National Insurance contributions you have made throughout your working life. DHSS leaflet NP32 'Your Retirement Pension' gives full details of contribution requirements and the types of pension now available. Basically, the number of qualifying years of NI contributions made during your working life determines what, if any, state pension you are entitled to. Important points that you may need to consider are:

- If you are a married woman and you elected to pay a reduced rate of National Insurance contribution you may not be able to claim a pension of your own on the basis of these contributions. Your pension would be linked to your husband's contributions.
- If you are the recipient of child benefit, or have to stay at home to look after a dependant, you will be protected (for those years) by 'home responsibilities protection'. This means that these years will be automatically deducted from the number of years required to qualify for a full pension instead of showing a gap in your record.
- If you are granted a 'certificate of exception' from paying National Insurance contributions on the grounds of small earnings (and you do *not* have 'home responsibilities protection' described above), your National Insurance record will not be credited during any period of exception and you may find your retirement pension reduced as a result.

You may also want to consider a personal pension plan, especially if you are the main earner in the family. If you are in employment and run your typing service on a spare-time basis you *may* belong to an occupational pension scheme. However, if you are totally self-employed you should consider one of the multitude of plans and policies available for the self-employed. Your insurance broker will be able to provide details of a number of different schemes and advise you on the most appropriate for your needs.

Pricing, costing and estimating

The financial plan you devised earlier (Chapter 2) should have given you an insight into your initial and recurring costs and provided a broad view of your anticipated earnings over several months. How are you going to convert that broad plan into the day-to-day costing of assignments?

Methods of charging

One of the first things you will have to decide is *how* to charge for your service. There are a number of conventional methods of charging depending as much on personal preference as the type of assignment, and there is no reason why you shouldn't adopt several methods depending on the circumstances and your customers' requirements.

Many typing services and most secretarial agencies charge an hourly rate. If you do this your customers will expect you to give them an estimate of the time it will take you to complete an assignment. You should take into account the complexity of the work (are there lots of tables; is the language very technical?) and the way it is being presented to you (is the handwriting very bad; will you be expected to reword it?) when estimating the time it will take you to complete it.

Almost all home-typists initially *under*estimate the time it will take to complete a task. Until you are more experienced and can produce fairly accurate estimates you should think about *doubling* your first estimate. Your customers will be happier (and more likely to use you again) if your estimates are realistic or even too high, than if they suddenly find themselves being charged twice as much as they expected because the assignment took longer than you anticipated.

For straightforward typing that is easy to read it should take you about one hour to type roughly 2000–3000 words (depending on your typing speed). You can estimate the number of words by counting the number on one line then multiplying by the number of lines per page times the number of pages. Add extra time if the writing is difficult to read, if there are tables or lots of tabulations involved, or if you have to correct spelling and grammar as you go along. Remember to allow time for proof-reading at the end, and perhaps for correcting any mistakes you make, as well as for any special requirements such as making photocopies, ruling up tables, stapling, providing envelopes, and so on. Finally, if you are charging by the hour, you will need some method of accurately recording the time spent working on a particular assignment.

Another popular method of charging is per page (this normally means per A4 page). You can operate a sliding system of charges depending on whether your customer wants double-line or single-line spacing and whether each page comprises only a small amount of typing (say a short invoice) or whether it is a complete page of text. Again you will need to be able to estimate how many pages a particular assignment is going to cover. This will depend on the customer's requirements, the type-face on your typewriter, and the margin settings you use. A good way of finding out how much typing you can get on to a page using *your* typewriter is actually to type out a few full pages in single-line and double-line spacing, as well as a few small sample invoices and letters (time yourself while you are doing this so that you can see how long particular assignments take you). You should then be able to estimate how many pages of typing will be produced by a particular assignment and provide your customers with a reasonably accurate idea of what the final charge will be.

Charging by the number of words (usually per 1000 or part thereof) is another useful method. One advantage of this method is that the onus is on your customer to make his own estimate of the likely charge (if he wants to know what the assignment will cost he can count the number of words himself). On the other hand unless you are using a word processor (which will calculate the number of words you are typing for you) *you* will have to count (or estimate) the number of words in the assignment in order to charge your customer. Another problem is that this method is not very appropriate for small assignments such as the odd letter or a small batch of invoices where the number of words might never reach 1000. In these circumstances you could use your rate per 1000 as a *minimum* rate per job, assignments of under 1000 words being charged the rate for 1000.

You can, of course, have a combined charging method depending on your customers' requirements and their appropriateness to the assignment in question. Dissertations and theses, for example, can usefully be charged per 1000 words (the student concerned will normally have a good idea of the number of words: dissertations usually come to between 8000 and 20,000 words; masters' and PhD theses up to about 80,000). Letters, invoices, leaflets and so on could be charged by the page or by the hour. Curricula vitae (CVs) could be charged per job, that is, a set charge covering the interview, construction of the CV, typing and producing a certain number of copies.

Another method which can be effective if you are working regularly for several small businesses (or overflow agencies) is to charge a set quarterly retaining fee and then a reduced hourly rate when any typing is required. In this way the business concerned knows that they have 'retained' your services and that you will be available to deal with any secretarial work as and when required and *you* are provided with a regular income in the form of the retaining fee. The disadvantage of this method is that you lose some of the potential flexibility that comes with a home-based typing service. Once you have accepted a retaining fee you *must* be prepared to take on work from that business source as and when they provide it. You can't decide to turn away typing work for a week while you decorate the house or go on holiday!

What will you charge?

The amount you actually charge will be a balance between your costs (and the time you put in) and the going rate for typing services in your area. You should have a good idea of what rates are being charged in your area if you followed the advice in Chapter 2. You should also ask yourself several other questions. How do the charges of other typing services relate to the service being offered? Are the typing services that are charging a higher rate offering a better service? How do other services compare with the one you are offering?

In addition, if you are adopting several methods of charging you will need to ensure that your rates per hour, per 1000 words and per page tally reasonably well, that is you would be charging roughly the same price for a dissertation whether you charged your hourly rate, your rate per 1000 words, or your rate per page. You can check this when you do a long piece of typing by timing yourself and then comparing this with your rates per 1000 words and per page.

Bearing in mind that town centre agencies invariably charge more than home-based typing services and that rates vary according to the area in which the service operates, hourly rates of between £2.00 and £6.00 are typical for home-based typing services and £4.00–£10.00 per hour for secretarial agencies. These rates are for straight typing. If you are offering additional services charge more.

One common fault with many home-based typing services is *undercharging*. While there may be advantages in launching your service with special cut-price rates in order to attract custom, there is no point in running a business that does not make any money! Because most types of 'home work' (especially for women) are grossly underpaid, it is all too easy to feel that your service is not *worth* very much to your customers. If you want to work ten hours a day for £1.00 per hour that is entirely up to you and you may be able to attract custom with such low prices – but you may also become quickly disheartened with your business if it provides such negligible financial rewards. Don't assume either that undercharging will necessarily bring you more customers. Statistics show that people are very wary of excessively low prices, equating them with lack of quality, poor goods, and shoddy service.

If you charge a little more than other typing services near you but have a more professional attitude and dedication to your service than your competitors, you will soon find customers queuing at the door and you will be reaping the rewards, both financial and psychological, of a properly run business.

Chapter 5

Sell Yourself! Marketing Your Service

Effective advertising is important for almost any business but it is especially crucial for a home-based typing service. You may be offering the best service in the country but if no one knows where you are, or what you can do, your business will never be a success.

Advertising

Advertising serves two purposes – to bring your service to the attention of your customers and to persuade them to use it. You will therefore need to ensure that you are using appropriate advertising methods in order to maximise both the number of potential customers who will find out about your service and the number who will be convinced that it is worth using.

Free promotion and advertising methods
Unfortunately, advertising is often quite expensive especially for a new service. However, there are many ways of getting your message across without actually spending any money!

Many local newspapers and local radio stations are interested in new businesses starting up in the area and may be happy to do an item on your service. The same is true of specialist magazines and journals who may be willing to insert a small editorial notice informing their readers that you have set up a typing service of special relevance to them.

Your Thomson local directory will be happy to give you a free insertion in both their classified and alphabetical sections (as well as some free stickers and leaflets telling people that you can be found in Thomson's). You can also have a more prominent advertisement providing details of the kind of service you are offering but you will be charged for this. Yellow Pages have a similar system, but will only allow a free entry for subscribers with a separate business telephone number. Again, larger advertisements are charged for. Details of whom to contact regarding insertions can be found in the relevant directory.

If you are planning to type dissertations, theses, essays, book manuscripts and so forth, a good method of 'free' advertising is to put up leaflets on the notice boards in colleges and universities near you. It is also worth leaving details of your service – neatly typed on an index card – with the administrative office of these establishments as many students, staff and even members of the public will contact the college or university office to enquire about typing services in the area.

Careful planning and construction should go into your notice. Don't simply scribble your name and address on a scrap of paper and pin it on the board under 'Typing Services'. Type your notice neatly and perfectly and make sure you include all the relevant details and information about the student service you are offering. Highlight special promotional features such as 'rapid turnaround', 'free copies', 'translations', 'correction of spelling and grammar', 'scientific and mathematical symbols available', plus any specialist terminology you understand. Use a bold heading to attract attention and don't forget to leave clear details of how and when you can be contacted. It is probably a good idea to give your rates – many students don't want the bother of telephoning several typists to compare rates and services and if your advertisement gives all the details they need and clearly states your policy on corrections and alterations (which can be fairly common in theses), how many copies are included, what special features you can offer and what your charges are, you should be able to attract a lot of custom from this quarter.

Another possible source of free advertising is to use the free notice boards provided by large stores and supermarkets. Some of these specifiy that 'trade' notices are not allowed but many will permit you to pin up one of your business cards or a small index card giving details of your services. This is a good way of promoting services of interest to the general public such as a letter writing service.

Shop window and post office notice boards

Putting up notices in shop windows and sub-post offices is a fairly cheap method of advertising. Most small shops charge about 10p to 30p per week to put up a notice in their window. Again, think carefully not only about *what* you are going to say on your notice but *which* shops will be the best to use. In general, people hardly ever need personal typing or secretarial services, but if you can put up notices near business or college areas you may be able to attract attention to your service for very little outlay. Town centre printing and copying shops, office suppliers and stationers may also be willing to allow you to put up a notice on their premises for a small charge. You may be able to convince a print and copy service to promote your business by agreeing to have all your copying and printing done by them.

Classified advertising

Advertising under the 'Business Services' section of your local newspaper is often a very effective method of attracting business. Many people – businessmen, students, writers and so on – look for typing services in the classified ads section. This *can* seem expensive, especially at first when your business has not really started to cover its costs, but a regular advertisement is often the most effective method of promoting a typing service. Most local newspapers offer a sliding scale of charges with reductions (or free insertions) if advertisements are run for more than one or two days. Don't make the mistake of advertising once a week for a month and then deciding that the method is useless because you have acquired hardly any customers this way! You will have much greater success if you run an ad every day for three months. This will be more expensive but it has been shown that this kind of advertising needs to be frequent and long term in order to achieve results.

The author proved this by running an advertisement twice a week for four weeks to which very little response was received (in fact the business acquired through this advertisement didn't even cover the cost of advertising), followed by the same advertisement every day for two weeks. At the end of the fortnight she was so inundated with work that she had to start turning people away!

The wording of classified advertisements is even more crucial than that of notices because you need to get your message across in a much more economical way. A large boxed advertisement will attract attention and is often useful at the beginning of your promotion. Use it again intermittently to remind people about your service. You can follow this with a smaller, regular, two or three line advertisement which will be much cheaper to run. The wording of your advertisement should be positive, in short sentences, and should stress the professionalism and quality of your service. The two examples below show how economy of words and a positive approach can produce a much better advertisement for the same cost.

Example 1.
Do you have typing or word-processing requirements? Experienced typist offers external secretarial services. Tel: Mrs S Smith (0101) 343434.

Example 2.
TYPING & WORD-PROCESSING. Speed and accuracy guaranteed. Collection and delivery, free copy, reasonable rates. Tel: Susie (0101) 343434 (24 hrs).

If you are offering a special service then make sure your advertisement appears in the appropriate classified section. People looking for a change of job will notice a CV production service advertised under 'Professional Vacancies', for example, while hopeless letter writers may notice an ad in the 'Personal Services' column.

A very specialised service (such as medical or legal typing) could be advertised effectively in an appropriate professional journal. Most of these have a classified advertisements section but their rates vary enormously. You will need to contact the classified section of the journal to ascertain their charges. Many areas of the country also have a free weekly advertising paper (often delivered to every household) which will carry your ad. The rates are usually very reasonable and your freesheet may have a greater circulation than the local daily newspaper. Nationwide daily newspapers are another possible channel for classified advertising, but their rates are generally *very* much higher than those of local papers. If you are offering a service that can usefully be operated through the postal system, then nationwide advertising could be a good idea. Again, you will need to advertise regularly and for an extended period in order to achieve substantial results. Because this form of advertising is relatively expensive, you want to be sure of recouping the cost through the business you generate from it. BRAD – *British Rate and Data* – a monthly publication which you should be able to obtain from your reference library, carries an exhaustive list of publications, advertising rates and circulation statistics. *Willing's Press Guide* and *Benn's Press Directory* provide even larger lists.

For further advice on constructing good advertisements and marketing you could try *Effective Advertising, The Daily Telegraph Guide for the Small Business* by H C Carter (Kogan Page) which provides a comprehensive coverage of all types of advertising for the small business and 'Marketing: A Guide for Small Firms' by E G Wood which is issued free by the Small Firms Service.

Direct mail shots

If you want to encourage small businesses to use your service a direct mail shot can be an effective way of reaching your customers. Unfortunately, the typical response for mail shots is usually fairly low. Only about 2 to 5 per cent of the people you contact are likely to show interest in your service which means that fairly large mailings are usually necessary.

You can either produce a suitable leaflet yourself and copy it or have a batch printed professionally (this will be more expensive, of course, but usually presents a much more 'professional' appearance). As with your notices and advertisements, the leaflet you send out directly to small businesses in your area should be well laid out and concise. Find out which local businesses are likely to need your service (their advertisements in the local paper, Thomson local directory and Yellow Pages will help) and make a list of these. If possible find out the name of the owner and address the mail shot to him or her personally (use a word-processor rather than a photocopier).

Remember to keep your message short and to the point. Managers of small businesses do not have the time to read through pages of print so keep the text down to one side of a small leaflet (say one A5 sheet). They are also likely to throw your leaflet straight into the bin after reading it, regardless of whether or not they might want to use your services later, so give them some incentive either to keep the leaflet (eg print a complimentary calendar on the back of it), or enclose one of your business cards (which is more likely to be kept for future reference), or even an easily completed reply-paid postcard which they can send off to receive further information or arrange an interview.

Emphasise the speed, accuracy, reliability and confidentiality of your service. Pinpoint the features which are likely to be of interest to small businesses, such as audio-typing, telephone dictation, collection and delivery, on-site filing and so on. Consider whether you could offer a more comprehensive service, for example a computer database facility for storing the records of a small business, bookkeeping or wages preparation. Perhaps you are prepared to work at your customers' premises for some of the time or would be prepared to 'fill-in' during holidays or sick-leave. It can also be fruitful to follow up a mail shot with a phone call a day or two later. This reminds the client of your service and gives you the opportunity to discuss his or her particular needs in relation to the service you can offer.

When mailing local groups, enclose your business card (several for a writers' society) and phone them the following week to ask if they would like to know any more about your service.

The major cost of a large scale mailing shot is likely to be postage. Delivering your leaflets by hand will overcome this cost but is usually only feasible if you have a fairly small area to cover and plenty of time in which to do it. (Remember that while you are out delivering leaflets you are not in to answer the telephone.) The Post Office do offer special rates for bulk deliveries. They also offer a free 'trial' mail shot delivery of 1000 leaflets to businesses that have never used a mail shot before and you can get a leaflet about this service from central post offices.

Word of mouth recommendation

The benefits of 'word of mouth' recommendation are incalculable. Most small-businessmen know others, writers know other writers, unemployed people needing CVs know others needing CVs, students wanting dissertations typed know other students in the same situation. If you provide a good service the chances are that your customers will tell other people about it and you will receive a lot of 'free' publicity and custom in this way.

Of course, you can also receive 'bad' publicity if your service is slow, if you make a lot of errors or if you are unfriendly. You should be aware of the importance of your reputation locally. A few shoddy assignments, a week of disorganisation because your typewriter has broken down or a grossly overpriced dissertation can seriously affect your business. Not only will your customer not return with further work but he will probably advise others not to use your service.

'Blowing your own trumpet' can also be very effective. Tell people about your service. Get them to pass on details to their friends or likely clients. Ask your customers how they came to find out about you. Do they know anyone else who might be interested in your service? Could you give them a business card for their friend?

Business cards

No matter how small your typing service, a batch of properly printed business cards is well worth the investment. Not only can you enclose these with direct mail shots and contact letters, but you can also leave supplies at your local copying shop, further education establishment, writers' society, and so on, as well as handing them out liberally to anyone and everyone. Carry several with you so that you can pin them up whenever a suitable notice board presents itself or hand one out whenever someone mentions the need of a typist.

Your business card needs to be attractive and informative. Try to indicate the range of your services without cramming too much on to the card. Your name, business name and telephone number are the obvious essentials. You may also like to include your address and a brief description of your service. For example:

SUSIE'S SECRETARIAL SERVICES

Typing, word-processing, computerized bookkeeping

Dissertations	Manuscripts
Business	Personal
Reasonable Rates	Rapid Turnaround

Contact: Susie Smith
1 Any Street
Anytown   Tel: (0101) 343434

Most printers will produce business cards. Ask to see some samples. They will help to formulate your ideas for your own business card. Try to get several quotations before deciding which printer to use – their rates can vary. You should be able to get an initial batch of 100 cards printed for about £15–£20 with reductions for batches of 500 and 1000 or more. Special reductions may be possible if you have headed stationery printed at the same time.

I think it can be a waste of money to have letterheads, invoices and other stationery printed while you are still operating your service from home. For the first year or so you should be able to manage perfectly well typing up your own letters and invoices – especially if you have a word-processor. Printing costs can run very high once you go beyond the business card stage. However, many typing services *do* have properly printed stationery and this has the advantage of looking really businesslike.

You may be able to cooperate with a local small printer. Many of these do not employ a professional typist and are often asked to typeset or produce documents (by typewriter) ready for photocopying or printing. You may be in a position to help each other: you by filling *their* need for an occasional typist, probably at a reduced rate, they by offering *you* special rates for your own (and your customers') printing needs.

Special offers

The most obvious time to offer a special rate is when you first start up your service. You want to attract customers who will (hopefully) be so impressed by your service that they will be happy to pay the 'normal' rate subsequently. One good way of promoting your service is to offer typing at half-price for the first month of business. You could also encourage small businesses to give you a try by offering to do one small 'free' assignment without obligation, followed by a reduced rate for the next month or so.

Marketing is more than simply selling your service

Good promotion of your service does not simply involve putting a few ads in the paper. You must be sure that your typing service is suitable for the market at which it is aimed. Is there a need that is not being filled? Can you offer something a little different that will attract custom to you rather than to the established services? Are you in a position to alter your strategy if you find the potential market is not as you anticipated.

A flexible approach is essential. You must be prepared to gear your typing service to the market that arises. For example, you might initially direct your service towards overflow work for local businesses with other typing as a sideline. But if your find you are actually being asked to prepare quite a lot of resumés, you may need to rethink your original policy and perhaps promote a comprehensive curriculum vitae service while retaining the overflow typing work as the sideline. Don't feel you have to stick to your original plan if there is obviously a better market to be had in a slightly different field.

Successful marketing therefore involves not only researching the typing market and your competitors in advance, but includes devising a sensible pricing policy that will allow you a realistic profit margin, adopting a flexible approach (at least for the first year), launching a well-planned advertising compaign and catering for a typing need that your competitors overlook.

Marketing does not stop once you have acquired a good supply of customers. If you want your service to remain successful you need to be constantly thinking of ways to improve it, ever watchful of new opportunities and new developments. Remember that *other* typing services will also be trying to compete with *you*. Don't allow complacency to turn what could be a very successful typing service into one that simply ticks over from day to day.

Your personal image

One final point to consider when promoting your business is the image you yourself present. Are you confident and outgoing? Do you quickly put people at ease? Are you able to direct a conversation and ask relevant questions without appearing rude? Can you maintain a professional and mature approach even under pressure, for example when several new clients turn up at once, or when a client disagrees with you?

The public image of your typing service will be as much influenced by your own personality and how well you can deal with people as by your qualifications and secretarial skills. This is especially true when dealing with customers over the telephone. For most typing services, the initial contact with any potential client is by telephone. Your customers will be extremely variable. Some will have a list of questions ready to ask you and have a very good idea of what is involved in their particular assignment. Others won't have the faintest idea where to start. You will need to be able to adapt to either type, providing relevant information quickly and efficiently in the first case and encouraging your contact to divulge his order needs and explaining how you can fill them in the second.

Once you are dealing with customers face to face you will need to maintain the professional image initiated over the telephone. Your manner and ability to deal efficiently with the necessities of ascertaining their requirements will be as influential as your ability to produce a high quality piece of typing.

The image of your typing service will also be enhanced by an attractive office. Your clients will be more impressed if you can interview them in a clean, tidy room where your samples, work-station, pens and paper are all to hand and obviously well organised than they will be if you interview them in an untidy living room with the baby climbing up your legs and the family cat sitting on a dusty typewriter in the middle of the dining table!

Chapter 6

Tools of the Trade

Setting up your office

Although a home-based typing service does not make great demands in terms of storage or work-space you should consider carefully *where* in your home to set up your office. A spare-room is obviously the ideal situation. Here you can have a desk, all your equipment to hand, plenty of storage space and, if your room is large enough, a clean and quiet area in which to receive your customers. Remember though that if you use the room *exclusively* for your typing service and claim it as a tax expense, you could be liable for capital gains tax when you sell your house.

Don't despair if you haven't got a separate room from which to operate your typing service. Very few home-based typing businesses do, especially in the initial stages. You *can* start a typing service using a walk-in cupboard as your office or even a desk or table in the corner of a room. You could work in your garden shed or use part of the garage or loft. One ingenious lady converted her understair 'glory hole' into a very neat 'mini-office': she installed an electric light and socket, shelves for her files, a fitted desk for her typewriter and a telephone extension.

While you are deciding which part of your home to use you should consider several factors:

1. Will you be able to leave your typewriter/equipment set up there, and will it be safe from interference by pets/children etc?
2. Will you have enough space to keep several files and books (dictionaries, address books etc) close to hand and safe?
3. Will you be able to work there at any time (when children are playing or in bed; when the television is on) or will you be restricted to certain hours? Remember, businessmen and students often want typing done at short notice, which may involve working during the evening or at weekends.
4. Will you be comfortable working there perhaps for several hours at a time? Cramped conditions, bad seating or

lighting and inconvenient access to files and books can be very draining, and will also slow you down.

You will also need to think about where to put all your equipment. A desk is not absolutely essential but you *will* need a large flat table-top on which to put your typewriter with enough space around it to rest other equipment such as your copy-holder, pencils, rubber, correction fluid and dictionary. You will need drawers (or some other storage device) in which to store paper, envelopes, ribbons and small equipment (paper clips, hole-punch, stapler, pens etc) and a place to store your customers' work safely both before and after it has been typed. A supply of manilla folders which can be stored in a lockable drawer is useful for this. You will need shelves as close as possible to your typing area for dictionaries, address books, files, accounting books, typing manuals and so on, and an area where your customers can sit comfortably, preferably with a table-top to rest on, to discuss their needs with you and to check the work when they come to collect it. You will also need a comfortable chair, at the correct height for your typewriter, to use when you are typing.

A final consideration when deciding on the location of your office is ease of access to the telephone. Once your business is moving you will find that you are receiving and making many phone calls a day. It can be frustrating to have to keep leaving your desk to trek through to the hall to answer the telephone every ten minutes. If you cannot reach the telephone without getting up from your desk you should seriously consider having an extension fitted. If you are already on the telephone it is not very expensive to have a simple socket extension fitted close to your desk and you can now purchase a British Telecom approved telephone which will plug into it for under £10.00.

Selecting and purchasing equipment

Once you have decided *where* you are going to operate your business you will have to decide *what* equipment you need to buy. This section covers your 'non-renewable' or 'capital' equipment needs. That is, equipment that is not actually used up as part of the business (except, of course, for normal wear and tear) such as your desk, typewriter, stapler, hole-punch, calculator and so on. These are the items that will appear as the 'assets' of your business in your annual balance sheet. Renewable supplies such as paper, envelopes, staples and so on are covered on page 78 – and these will be included as 'expenses' on your profit and loss account.

Furniture and fittings

There is very little point in rushing out and buying a brand new office desk when you first set up your typing service. These are unnecessarily expensive and often far too large and cumbersome to fit comfortably into a small room. You *can* use a spare table (preferably one that you can fit drawers or a filing cabinet underneath) but make sure that it is a suitable height for typing. Most dining tables are too high to type at comfortably. If you are trying to keep costs down you can actually make a desk by resting a smooth door on breeze-blocks, a pair of old bedside cabinets or a pair of two-drawer filing cabinets.

If you are going to invest in a desk consider either a second-hand office or teacher's desk or one of the do-it-yourself variety that comes in kit form. A second-hand office desk that is in good condition is probably the best buy as it will be strong and durable and of better quality than a 'kit' type desk. You should also be able to sell it later on for much the same price as you pay for it provided you keep it in good condition. Many office suppliers can provide second-hand office desks. Alternatively, look in the classified ads under 'Office Equipment'. You should find a number of firms selling off old office equipment. Another good source of quality second-hand desks is auction sales – either purely office furniture auctions or general auction sales. Most large towns have an auction saleroom with auctions once or twice a week; these will be advertised in the local press.

When you go out in search of your desk take a tape-measure with you and the measurements of your room. You need to be sure that you can accommodate it. Decide beforehand whether you want a single pedestal desk, one with drawers at both sides, one with a built-in filing cabinet at one side and drawers at the other, or whatever. Make sure that the drawers slide in and out easily and the desk stands solidly without rocking when pushed. Run your hand across the top. Is the surface smooth or does it have grooves or splinters that will make writing difficult? Is the top large enough to be used both as a typewriter stand *and* as a writing surface or would you be better with a small writing desk and separate typewriter stand?

What about a filing cabinet? Although these are very useful, especially once your business is established, they do tend to be rather expensive, especially new ones. If you can get an office desk with a built-in single-drawer filing cabinet at one side this will probably suffice. You can get a two-drawer 'kit' type filing cabinet for about £40.00 new, and a steel four-drawer filing cabinet for about £70.00. Again, buying second-hand is probably the answer. Unfortunately, second-hand filing cabinets are rarely in such good condition as second-hand desks. Small dents in the front and sides don't really matter so long as they don't interfere with the sliding drawer mechanism or the lock, and you can brighten up a chipped grey filing cabinet with bright paint. Make sure the drawers slide in and out easily and the file hanging runners (inside the drawers) are intact and not rusting or bent.

You will also need shelf space on which to store books, directories and manuals. If you don't already have shelving you can construct cheap shelves yourself using planks of wood supported by bricks, or buy shelf-making kits. The ideal place for shelves is over or next to your desk so that you can reach your files and books without having to leave your seat.

A comfortable chair is another essential. Don't skimp on this or you will pay for it with backache and a stiff neck. It is well worth investing in a proper typist's chair. This should have an adjustable back rest, adjustable height and preferably a swivel base and wheels. Again, it is possible to buy these second-hand, but test them out carefully as most second-hand office chairs really are on their last legs! With the advent of home-computing, many modern furniture retailers are now selling 'computer operators' chairs' at a fraction of the cost of a new 'office' model. These are not quite so well made but can be substantially cheaper. Go for one with cloth rather than vinyl on the seat. Vinyl is prone to splitting and can become rather uncomfortable in hot weather!

Lighting is also important. If you haven't got a good overhead light above your desk then you will need to invest in an angle-poise reading lamp. These are not expensive, but make sure you can use at least a 60W bulb in the lamp and that you will have adequate space to erect it so that it shines on to your work from the side or behind you. Don't make do with a table lamp or work in a dim corner of the room. You will be slowed down by eye-strain and lack of concentration if you cannot see the copy or typescript clearly.

Office equipment

How much additional equipment you buy will be determined by the kind of service you intend to operate and how much you want to spend. Larger items such as telephone answering machines, copiers, word-processors, transcribers and so on are dealt with in the next chapter. The purchase of your typewriter is dealt with below. However, you will also need several small items of equipment if your service is to run smoothly and easily.

A hole-punch will be useful not only for your own filing but when your customers request that documents are punched ready for filing. Buy a strong punch with at least two hole settings and as large a gap for paper insertion as possible. It can be frustrating to have to punch a sheaf of papers in two batches because your punch-hole will not take more than two or three sheets at a time. A punch that has guide markings to show you where to position the paper is very useful, especially if you have to punch many pages accurately.

A stapler is another essential piece of equipment. You may already have a small pocket stapler but this is unlikely to be suitable for a typing service. In general, the larger the stapler the more sheets of paper you can fasten together with it. Choose a sturdy model that has rubber grips on the bottom (so that you don't scratch your desk and it doesn't slip while you're stapling) and make sure that you can get staples for it locally – preferably in large boxes. A hand-stapler should suffice but if you are likely to be doing large amounts of stapling you might need to consider buying an electrically powered model. These are very quick and can staple more sheets together than hand-staplers but they are rather expensive – don't buy one unless you absolutely need to.

Although it is not essential, you should also consider buying a copy-holder. This is a device which holds work for copy-typing and is usually adjustable so that the work is supported at a height and angle that is easy to read without having to turn your head very far or lean over. Most people, even in offices, actually manage without these, but they can save a touch-typist quite a bit of time and annoyance. You don't have to peer around your typewriter or try to read poor handwriting at a strange angle! Copy-holders with either a desk stand or an extension arm that clamps to the edge of the desk can be purchased for under £20. Some models have a movable magnifying cursor which moves up and down the text according to your current typing line.

Another non-essential but highly recommended item is a pocket calculator. If you are working for accountants or businesspeople they may want you to perform some calculations for them or check figures before typing. Even if you don't need a calculator for your work you will find your own bookkeeping, invoicing and estimating are quicker and easier if you use a calculator. You can get a simple model that will perform basic functions (addition, subtraction, multiplication and division) for a few pounds. If you are doing a significant number of calculations for customers, you might need to invest in a larger desk-top calculator that produces a printout. Don't buy one of these until you are *sure* that you really need it – the cheapest models start at about £20 and perform only basic functions as well as producing a printout.

Apart from having a place to *store* supplies of paper, ribbons and so on, you may well need to have a readily accessible supply on or near your desk top. A small paper-holder which can be fitted to one wall or stand on the corner of your desk is very useful. These usually have several 'shelves' and can hold a small supply of paper (top and copy), carbon paper, envelopes, customers' headed paper and so on.

You may require other small items such as a waste basket, Sellotape dispenser, postage scale, bulletin board, scissors, staple remover and so on. A checklist of start-up supplies appears at the end of this chapter. You may not need to buy all of these items: beware of making unnecessary or rash purchases of equipment you may never need to use.

All the above equipment can be purchased at stationers or office suppliers. Make a list of your needs and compare the prices and models available in several shops before you decide on your purchases. And remember to keep all your receipts.

Selecting a typewriter

This is probably your most crucial piece of equipment. Having the right typewriter for your own preference and requirements is essential to the smooth operation of your business.

The kind of typewriter you purchase will depend on how extensive your service will be and what kind of typing work you will be doing. If you are only planning to spend a few hours per day typing forms and envelopes then you should be able to manage very well with a portable manual typewriter. However, if your work-load is more extensive than this you will almost certainly need to invest in an office-size electric or electronic typewriter. There are so many different models available that you should consider carefully the particular features that your typing service will require. Before you rush off to buy your typewriter make a checklist of all the features that suit you best.

Some typewriters use only film *or* fabric ribbons. Film ribbons, also known as carbon ribbons, produce an excellent, crisp, finish but are expensive because they can only be used once. Many models use both film *and* fabric ribbons and this allows greater flexibility. You might also need to check whether you can acquire ribbons in colours other than black: you may need a red ribbon, for example, if you do a lot of work for an accountant. Another point to consider is the ease with which ribbons can be changed: some models require fiddly threading of ribbon between spools, others have a cartridge or quick change system. While you are looking at these features find out how much the ribbons cost and whether these are available locally. Ribbon prices can also vary considerably from model to model.

Many electric typewriters now incorporate a self-correcting device. This produces a much neater correction than the traditional rubbing out or correction fluid method and is very much faster. Self-correcting typewriters use film ribbons together with a correcting ribbon which lifts off the incorrect letter(s) allowing you to re-type the correct one(s). A three-stage process is involved which is actually very fast once you get the hang of it. You strike the 'correction key', then type the error letter(s), then type in the correct letter(s). On some models you have to actually take out the film cartridge and replace it with the correction cartridge during this process which is somewhat inconvenient, but most models allow you to have the film and correction ribbons in the machine simultaneously.

You should also consider whether you require a long carriage, interchangeable elements (which allow you to use various type styles as well as mathematical and scientific symbols, music, foreign languages etc) variable spacing (horizontal and vertical) and so on. A model that has a horizontal half-space key will allow you to insert missing letters. One with a vertical half-space key will be useful if you need to type subscripts and superscripts (students and writers often need this feature). The cost of new elements, ribbons and spare parts should also be taken into account. Check also whether you will be able to have your typewriter serviced and repaired locally.

Electronic typewriters are usually slightly more expensive than electric models and offer a range of features that is intermediate between a simple electric typewriter and a word processor. Electronic typewriters 'remember' the last few lines typed, allowing you to make corrections quickly and easily. Most have a range of 'automatic' features such as centring, underlining, paragraph indentation, alignment of columns, bold print, carriage return and so on. Some have a small screen which allows you to see the text you are typing before it is printed. There are also models that can 'store' frequently used phrases (or addresses) allowing you to type them at the touch of a button, while at the upper end of the market are the editable electronics which provide a basic form of word processing. Unlike electric typewriters which have either metal arms or 'golfball' type printing devices, electronic typewriters are normally equipped with a 'daisy wheel'. This is a revolving wheel with spokes radiating from its centre, each capped with a character. The wheel spins at high speeds, typing characters on to the page. Like the ball-type elements, daisy wheels are usually interchangeable, allowing you to provide a variety of typefaces and symbols. Electronic typewriters are generally very simple to use and can certainly speed up your output. They also tend to need less maintenance than electric typewriters because they have fewer moving parts but you may find it difficult to get them repaired locally.

An excellent, and strongly recommended guide to currently available typewriters is *A Handbook of New Office Technology* by J Derrick and P Oppenheim (Kogan Page) which gives a comprehensive coverage of the range and variety of machines available.

Whatever kind of typewriter you buy or hire you should thoroughly test it before you take it. You will want to be especially careful if you are buying second-hand.

Insert a sheet of paper in the machine, ask to be left alone for a few minutes, and check the following:

Type impression and touch. Try out each key (in both lower and upper case). The copy should be clear and regular at the 'average' impression setting. Make sure there are no 'light' and 'dark' impressions and that the touch is even over all the keys.

Alignment. Type a few rows of Is and Zs (iZiZiZiZ IzIzIzIz). The bottoms of these letters should all lie on the same plane. Try a few other combinations to ensure all the letters fall in the correct line.

Repeat keys and underlining. Make sure all the repeat keys work and that it takes extra effort to engage them. A repeat key that engages too easily will cause problems when you're typing, as will one that is too stiff. Underline some typing. Does the key start and stop when *you* want it to? Is the line uniform?

Space bar. This should have a light touch and advance the carriage only one space. A repeating space bar should require a much deeper press to engage it.

Backspace. Ensure that the backspace key always moves one full space when completely depressed. Check that any half-space mechanism advances or backspaces the carriage by the correct amount.

Double and triple spacings. Select alternative line spacings and type a few lines using these. The paper shouldn't slip and the spacings should be even.

Tabs. Set the tabs every ten spaces across the page and type a letter at each stop for a few lines. This will show whether the tab stops where it should each time. Ensure that tabs can be set and cleared easily.

Margin release. Type to the right-hand margin stop (the bell should ring audibly about seven spaces before the stop). Release the margin and type on – the letter spacing should remain uniform.

Carriage return. An automatic carriage return should work smoothly and immediately and return the carriage fully. It should not be so vigorous as to jerk the machine about on the table.

Feed rollers. Type a row of letters across the top, middle and bottom of a sheet. Roll back to the top and repeat the process typing over the first rows. The letters should land exactly over the first ones. If they don't you'll have difficulty making corrections.

Platen. This should be smooth, not cracked, and should 'give' slightly when depressed by a pencil point (it should spring back at least partially).

Service and maintenance are important considerations. Do consider asking for a service agreement. This usually consists of regular inspections and cleaning, replacing worn parts and service calls. Depending on the machine, service contracts range from about £20 to £100 per year. If you use the machine a lot, seven hours per day or more, this is probably well worth the money. However, you should consider whether it wouldn't make more sense to pay for parts and labour when you need them if your machine suffers less wear than this. Check that any service agreement covers both parts and labour and that you will be given a temporary replacement in the event of your machine being taken away for repair. A service and replacement agreement is normally included automatically in a leasing scheme.

If you want to get the best from your machine you should also have your own programme of cleaning and maintenance. Clean the type-bars frequently (but gently), never type on the platen when there is no paper in the machine and keep it moist and supple with platen cleaning fluid. Always cover your typewriter when not in use to keep dust out and try not to let rubber dust, or anything else for that matter, fall into the machine.

Renewable supplies

Renewable supplies include all things that will be 'used up' by your typing service. Although you will want to have an adequate range and quantity of supplies to deal with your work-load, you should not make the mistake of purchasing in bulk too soon. Start off with a small stock and increase it if you find you are using it up too quickly.

Buy your paper in reams (500 sheets) rather than smaller quantities as it is much cheaper. Start off with one ream of a good quality A4 general typing paper: Croxley Script 85g/m^2 is very suitable. You will also need a ream of white or coloured bank for copies and it is a good idea to have a ream of 80g/m^2 copier paper (not the shiny surfaced variety) for drafts. Copier paper is about half the price of 'proper' typing paper but is very similar in quality and perfectly adequate for drafts and carbon copies.

If you will be producing CVs or typing 'executive' letters using your own paper, you may also need to invest in a small quantity of high quality paper (100g/m^2). A full ream will be extremely expensive; W H Smith, for example, supply a 50-sheet pack of 'Deluxe Typing Paper' for about £2.35. By the way, if you are asked to use a more expensive paper you should make sure your charges are increased sufficiently to cover the cost. It is unlikely that you will be required to use anything other than A4 (297 × 210mm) except for legal documents or accounts, when your client may provide the correct paper for you, but a supply of A5 paper (half the size of A4) is useful for your own invoices and estimates.

You will also need a variety of envelopes in a range of standard sizes. Unless you do a lot of envelope stuffing, 200 size 9 × 4in and 50 size 9 × 12in should suffice initially. Buy other sizes and extra supplies as needed.

Carbon paper in appropriate sizes and colours will be required if you are to produce carbon copies and you will also need to purchase a supply of paper clips (assorted sizes), staples, Sellotape, typewriter ribbons, correction fluid (plus thinner) and/or ribbons, a typewriter rubber, pens, pencils (and sharpener), a ruler, jotters (you can make these yourself using the clean side of draft paper), postage stamps (first and second class to start with) and rubber bands. Buy all of these things in fairly small quantities at first and build up supplies as your work-load increases. Do remember to get and keep receipts for everything and write these purchases in your cash book straight away.

Checklist of start-up supplies

The following checklist is for guidance only: it is highly unlikely that you will need (or want) to purchase all the things on this list. Use it selectively. Space has been left for you to include any items not on the list. Tailor your requirements to suit your own typing service, needs and financial constraints. Shop around for the best value. Adding on any other initial expenses (eg advertising launch, printing business cards or office decoration) will give you a good idea of your initial costs.

	£		£
Desk	....	Calculator	
Filing cabinet	....	Dictionary	....
Shelves	....	Thesaurus	....
Typewriter	....	Waste basket	....
Word processor	....	Stapler (+	
Photocopier	....	staples)	....
Answering		Hole-punch	....
machine	....	Petty cash box	....
Dictation		Sellotape	
equipment	....	dispenser (+	
Telephone (or		Sellotape)	....
extension)	....	Manilla folders	....
Copy-holder	....	Sample display	
Typists chair	....	book	....
Computer		Ring binders	....
equipment:		Accounts books	....
....	....	Desk diary	....
....	....	.Report binders	....
....	....	Typing paper	....
Telex equipment		....	
(+ subscription)	....	....	
Facsimile		Envelopes	....
equipment	....	Carbon paper	....
Desk lamp	....	Ribbons	....
Others:		Correction fluid/	
....	....	erasers/correction	
....	....	ribbons	....
....	....	Address book	....
....	....	Sundries: paper	
....	....	clips, pens,	
....	....	rubber bands,	
....	....	postage stamps,	
....	....	jotters etc	....

TOTAL START-UP COSTS

£

Chapter 7

More Tools, More Trade

Once your business is established you may need to upgrade or expand your equipment. If you find yourself trekking to your local copy-shop more than once a week you might want to consider having your own photocopier. If you are constantly being interrupted by telephone calls from customers you might find an answering machine useful. A word processor will be a boon if you are frequently asked to type initial drafts which then have to be retyped as finished copy once alterations have been made. This chapter outlines some of this office technology which is now well within the grasp of most small businesses and may well be a lucrative asset to yours. Again, *A Handbook of New Office Technology* (Kogan Page) provides a very extensive coverage of current office equipment and is recommended for those desiring a more comprehensive overview.

Word processors

Although word processors are generally rather more expensive than electric (or electronic) typewriters they are infinitely more versatile. If your business is a full-time affair, if you find you are often asked to retype work or produce a preliminary draft, or if you have to type repetitive letters, hundreds of labels and so on, a word processor may be a really cost-effective investment.

The basic components of a word processor are a standard qwerty typewriter keyboard plus special 'function' and 'control' keys; a visual display unit (a screen on which you see the text prior to printing); a central processing unit (which enables the equipment to carry out automatic functions such as editing, storage and retrieval); a printer (on which the finished product will be produced); and some sort of storage/retrieval mechanism (usually a disc drive) which allows you to 'store' text for future use (see figure opposite). It may also use discs to program the word processor. Most word processors are supplied with an instruction package which teaches you how to use your particular model. If you've never used (or even seen) a word processor before, don't be put off by their apparent complexity. With a little time and patience you will find they are really very easy to operate and a great improvement on both electric and electronic typewriters! If you are still doubtful, you could enrol on a short word processing course (these are run in most towns) to get the feel of using one before you decide whether or not to buy.

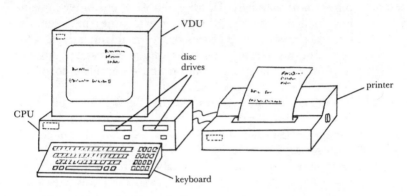

The Basic Components of a Word Processor

Don't think you can't afford one. Although the larger well-known office models are still quite expensive (usually £2000 or more) they have fallen dramatically in price and you can now get a perfectly good word processor for under £1000. The Amstrad PCW 8256, for example, is currently retailing for less than £400, and is an excellent machine for the home-typist. The updated Amstrad PCW 8512 which has a second disc drive and greater memory retails for under £500.

Word processors have several features which will speed up and improve the efficiency of your service:

(a) They allow you to see, alter and correct text as you type it and *before* it is finally printed. You can quickly insert, delete, copy or move any amount of text quickly and easily.

(b) They can (if you wish) automatically produce straight right *and* left margins to your work.

(c) They can 'store' text so that if your customer comes back with revisions, these can be made quickly and easily and *without retyping the whole document*.

(d) Many can produce subscripts, superscripts, symbols, footnotes and various type-faces at the push of a button.

81

(e) Frequently used expressions, addresses and names can be stored and automatically typed when required. Standard letters can also be stored together with a list of recipients' names and addresses, allowing you to get on with something else while your printer types them out for you.

(f) They have a search (or search and replace) facility which allows you to locate (or locate and change) a word or phrase automatically. If, for example, a customer finds he has spelled a name wrongly several times in a lengthy document, your word processor will go through the text for you, finding and altering the name as necessary. All you have to do is to press a button and a complete corrected copy will be printed automatically.

(g) They can number pages, justify paragraphs, tabulate, centre and underline, produce bold or normal print (and sometimes a range of other type-faces) all at the touch of a button.

(h) Dictionary programs are available which will go through the text checking and correcting spelling mistakes (and many typographical errors) in your script. These can save time during proof-reading and can be amended to include any unusual words or names that you use frequently.

(i) Many can rearrange lists alphabetically, selectively retrieve and organise stored data and have a range of business programs available that will allow you to offer a 'computerised' accounting/bookkeeping/filing/database/ invoicing/payroll service if you so desire.

Although word processors often come as a 'package' you may have a choice of printers. There are basically two types of printer, *impact* and *non-impact*. For economic reasons impact printers are currently the most popular among individuals and small businesses. There are two types: dot matrix and daisy wheel. Dot-matrix printers form letters using tiny dots. They are very versatile and can produce graphics (charts and diagrams) as well as a wide variety of text styles. If you decide on one of these make sure you purchase one that has a facility for producing 'near-letter quality' (NLQ) print. On a good printer this should be almost indistinguishable from true 'type-print' because the dots are so close together. The accepted standard for an NLQ printer is one with at least an 18-pin print head. Daisy-wheel (or 'letter quality') printers generally cost more and print more slowly; however, the quality of the print is far superior to that of NLQ on dot-matrix printers. Be guided by your needs. If you type predominantly theses, business correspondence and legal drafts, your customers will prefer the quality of a daisy-wheel printer. If you are frequently asked to intermix type-faces, need to produce graphs or lots of rough drafts then consider one of the cheaper, faster and very versatile dot-matrix printers.

Non-impact printers are quiet, fast, and produce a superior quality print. They are, however, comparatively expensive. *Ink jet* printers spray ink on to the paper at about 90 characters per second and can be obtained for around £500 + while *laser* printers (which are now selling at below £2000 for a desk-top model) use a laser beam to print characters and can also produce graphics. Some companies offer combined laser printer/photocopiers, for example the Xerox 4045 which retails for about £5000.

An alternative to buying a dedicated word processor is to buy a computer, a printer and word-processing program. This *can* work out more cheaply but you will have to shop around to get the best and cheapest combination. One recent offer, for example, was for a brand new, fully guaranteed Philips P2010 computer, plus Wordstar and Calcstar programs, and a Silver Reed EXP400 daisy-wheel printer for under £500 (mrp £1695).

One advantage of this set up is that it allows you to use a much greater range of business software and thus offer a much more comprehensive service to your customers. You will need a computer that has a standard qwerty keyboard and 'feels' good to type on. It will also need to have a fairly large memory (64K or more) in order to accommodate a word-processing program *and* a reasonable amount of text. You will need a visual display unit or VDU (sometimes called a monitor) and a printer (dot matrix or letter quality) that is compatible with your chosen computer. Make sure that it will take standard A4 typing paper. You will also need to check out the word-processing programs that are available for your computer. Most of the major micro-computers now have a range of word-processing and business software available. Make sure you buy the one that is the most suitable for your needs. The only disadvantage with this set-up is that your family might want to use your work-station to play computer-games, so beware!

Another possibility is to get one of the upgrades which converts an electronic typewriter into a fairly basic word processor by adding a VDU and disc drives. The only real disadvantage with this set-up is that the total cost will be close to that of a micro-computer, printer and word-processing software. And the latter constitutes a much better product.

There are very few disadvantages with word processors. They may be expensive, but rarely cost more than a good electric typewriter. However, it may be more difficult to have repairs and regular maintenance carried out on them. Check this with your supplier before you buy. You don't want to be left without a machine for several weeks while your word processor is being repaired.

Another possible problem is the eye-strain that some people experience when they have to watch a VDU for a long period of time. This problem can be reduced by fitting an anti-glare screen which retails for about £20. People who suffer from epilepsy or migraine may find that operating a VDU aggravates the condition. There has also been some concern about radiation from VDU screens but most medical authorities believe that the risks are minimal and certainly no more than would be present from prolonged watching of a colour TV or using a microwave.

You will also have to be more careful with a word processor or computer than you would be with a typewriter. If you spill your coffee on it, or on one of the discs or cassettes, you may seriously damage your equipment and lose hundreds of pages of text.

A final point worth taking into consideration is the cost of storage discs (or cassettes) and of ribbons for the printer. Printer ribbons are often more expensive than typewriter ribbons and may not be so easy to obtain. Check up on this before you buy.

Further information can be found in *So You Think Your Business Needs a Computer* by Khalid Aziz (Kogan Page).

Copiers

Next to a word processor, a photocopier is probably the greatest asset to any typing service. Whoever you are typing for, they will almost certainly want at least one copy of the work. Carbon copies are cheap but typing mistakes show (or take time to correct). Running off extra copies on a printer usually takes longer and is more costly than photocopying, as well as taking up valuable printing time that could be used for something else. Getting copies from a copying-centre is expensive, time-consuming and inconvenient.

Photocopies are quick and easy to produce, look more professional than carbon copies and are usually cheaper (for you) than printing or typing several copies of an assignment.

There are other advantages in having your own photocopier. Being able to take a copy of the original or only copy of a manuscript can be useful as a precaution against loss or damage. In addition, if your customer has a copy of your assignment it makes it easier for you to telephone him with any questions since you can refer to specific pages and line numbers. A photocopier will also be of use in your own work. You can produce your own stationery, advertisements, leaflets and price-lists. And you may also be able to enhance your service by offering photocopying as an extra facility.

To determine whether the purchase (or lease) of a photocopier would be feasible for your typing service you should consider:

- How many photocopies you currently get per month from a copy-centre
- What these copies cost
- How much time you spend travelling to/from and at the copy-centre
- How much it costs you to get to and from the copy-centre
- Whether you will advertise photocopying as an extra service
- Whether a photocopier would simply pay for itself (ultimately) or whether you would want it to make a profit in its own right
- What kind of copier would best suit your needs
- What your copier will cost to buy (or lease) and run

The cost, size and variety of photocopiers has changed considerably in the last ten years. You can now get machines small enough to sit on the corner of your desk as well as a wide range of stand-alone models.

Very broadly, there are two types of photocopier: those which feature specially coated paper with a 'dry' or 'wet' toner (wet systems are being rapidly phased out) and the 'plain paper' or 'xerographic' copier. Coated paper comes in rolls or cut sheets and has a slick feel compared with plain paper. It is unlikely to be acceptable to students, can usually only be copied on one side, is subject to greater deterioration and cracking than plain copier paper (which is ordinary office bond quality) and is usually more expensive. Hence a plain paper copier is recommended if you can get one.

To decide what type of copier you should buy you will need to determine your copying needs. This will include not only the number of copies you need per day (on average) but also any special requirements such as reduction or enlargement, double-sided copying, large runs (over 50 copies per run), and so on. You will need to consider not only the cost of the copier but also the cost and availability of supplies (toner, paper, developer, spare parts) and service.

At the cheaper end of the market are the desk-top copiers. Beware of buying anything too cheap and simple. Many of the simple desk-top models can only take *one* photocopy at a time and you may have to replace the original each time you take a copy. These copiers are unlikely to be suitable for a typing service. On the other hand, you can now get compact desk-top models which can produce multiple copies (usually up to 99 at a time) in a range of sizes for between £400 and £1000. The Selex 55, for example, produces 15 copies per minute and can handle every type of paper from A5 to A3.

Virtually all stand-alone models print multiple copies and use a range of paper sizes. You will pay more for a machine that can also reduce/enlarge, sort, collate, provide automatic page and line numbering, print in colour or re-format pages. Bear in mind that, although a brand new stand-alone model may be very expensive to buy, you can hire photocopiers or get good second-hand or reconditioned models (Xerox, for example, lease photocopiers and provide a good service/maintenance back-up; they also have a wide range of cheaper reconditioned models for hire or sale).

There is a range of special features available in some copiers which you may or may not need. Among recent innovations are photocopiers that can produce more than 150 copies per minute, automatically produce and collate 10,000 copies of large documents, print out a copy in any one of ten languages, produce 'negative' images, memorise frequently used copying jobs and do just about anything apart from make the tea! You are unlikely to need, or be able to afford, any of these features as yet. However, some of the less costly additional features you may need are outlined below.

If you regularly need to take on average more than one copy from any one original you may need a copier that can take *multiple copies*. On some models you can set the copy counter, push the start button and wait for your copies. On others, athough advertised as taking 'multiple copies', you have to re-insert the original for each additional copy. This defeats the object of having a multiple copy machine to some extent, since you cannot leave the machine and get on with something else while your photocopies are being made. Some models leave the original in place but only take one copy at a time: you have to push the print button for every copy. If you make more single copies than anything else, one of these simpler, and usually cheaper, models will suit your purpose. However, for a few hundred pounds more you might be able to purchase a machine which will be of greater use to your business in the *future*.

If you want to be able to make copies of books or other bulky items you will need to have a *lift-top* model. On some models you feed your original in one side and it is ejected, with the copy, at the other. Other models have a lift-up top and a glass plate on which the original has to be placed prior to printing.

Two-sided printing saves paper and is useful for leaflets and for reducing bulk. Most plain paper copiers can print on both sides of the paper manually (*you* have to turn the sheets over and re-insert them the other way up) and some do it automatically.

Many copiers (including some desk-top models) allow you to take *multiple-size copies*, usually A3 and A4. Some have two paper trays which hold paper of different sizes, allowing you to change the size of your paper by simply pushing a button; on others you have to remove one tray and insert the other for different sized copies.

A *document feeding* device holds a stack of originals, automatically feeds them into the copier and ejects them. This is only available on certain models but can be very useful if you often have to take a copy of a large manuscript.

Reduction and enlargement capacities will allow you to reproduce originals in a range of sizes. This may be useful if you need to reduce tables or diagrams for dissertation students or if you need to enlarge documents or tables for use on posters or for the partially sighted.

Most copiers incorporate a feature which allows you to select an appropriate *exposure setting* for the work so that you can get similar results from a very dark, normal or very pale original. They usually have a range of indicators which tell you when the machine is 'warmed up' ready for use, when you need to add paper and if there is a paper jam or other problem. Other controls generally include a dial or digital display showing the number of copies selected and a 'stop' key which allows you to override the machine and stop a copy run if a problem is encountered.

Once you have decided what kind of copier will best suit your needs you will need to think about whether buying (either new or reconditioned) or hiring will be better for you. In general, the very simple desk-top models are not offered for hire and are usually relatively cheap to purchase (£100–£300). For slightly more sophisticated models you may get a choice.

Although buying outright means that your costs are fixed and you have a valuable asset which you can sell later, hiring a copier will allow you to opt for a bigger machine as your business grows, and service is included in the hire charge. Hiring also gives you the option of changing your mind later on if you find that the costs of operating your own copier are not met by the profit you receive from its use.

Here are a few tips on getting good results from your plain paper copier. Using a film ribbon in your typewriter will give you clearer and darker photocopies. Dirty marks and smudges on the original can be masked with correction fluid but make sure it is dry before you position it on the glass plate. If you are making your original with paste-ups, stick the various portions to a piece of clean, white paper using glue or double-sided sticky tape: the edge of ordinary Sellotape usually produces a shadow-line on the photocopy. If you need to use guide lines, draw these with light green, light blue or yellow pencil – these colours do not show on the printed copy. Copy in black or red on white or pale yellow paper will produce the best results.

Transparent originals or those typed on both sides of lightweight paper do not photocopy well: use a good quality opaque paper and type on one side only for good copies.

Dictating machines

If you work for a number of small businesspeople who have very little time to sit down and write out correspondence, you might want to consider investing in a dictating machine. These are also useful for writers and students or for people who make recordings of interviews for subsequent typing.

Dictating machines come in a range of shapes and sizes. Some use standard-sized cassette tapes, others use special cassettes called mini- or micro-cassettes. There are two main components: the dictating unit (which your customer uses for recording) and the transcription unit (which you use to play back the recording). The transcription unit usually incorporates rewind, play, fast forward, stop and erase buttons and has a counter to indicate your position on the tape. It will have a headset (a lightweight earphone system) which allows you to listen to the recording in private and a pedal which allows you to start, stop and rewind the recording without touching the transcription unit. In some systems the dictating unit and the transcription unit are one, a microphone being added when recordings have to be made. This is unlikely to be a very useful system for a typing service, even if you are only providing audio-typing for one client, because only one of you can have the machine at a time. If your client has the machine for dictation, you cannot use it for transcription; when your client returns the machine to you for transcription he no longer has a facility for dictation! Either buy a machine that uses standard cassettes and let your customers provide their own facilities for recording, or invest in a system that uses fairly cheap portable dictating machines, usually with mini-cassettes which you can provide for your clients, and a compatible transcriber which remains on your premises.

The operation of a transcribing machine is very straightforward. You insert your customer's pre-recorded tape and rewind to the beginning. After setting up your typewriter you press the pedal to play the tape and listen to the recording through the headset. You release the pedal to type what you have just heard and press again to listen to some more. The system automatically backs up a little when you release the pedal so that you don't miss words when you begin typing again.

If you are regularly asked to type from standard cassettes you might consider buying a transcriber that takes standard cassettes. Alternatively, if you work for a number of small businesses which require a more portable system, you could buy a transcriber that uses mini- or micro-cassettes and supply your customers with a pocket-sized dictating machine and cassettes. These record about 30 minutes of dictation and, as with standard cassettes, can be erased and reused many times before they need to be replaced. If you use the latter system, make sure you erase the tapes before sending them out for reuse.

Telephone answering machines

Once your business is established you may find that you are constantly being interrupted by customers on the telephone. This not only reduces your efficiency, but can be an irritation when you are trying to get an urgent typing assignment completed. You may also be losing custom while you are out because there is no one to answer the telephone. Your regular customers are unlikely to be put off by an answering machine, especially if they know you will come back to them quickly, but it would not be very wise to use one all the time. A potential new customer calling to enquire if you can fit in an urgent assignment will probably try elsewhere if met by an answering machine (and it has to be admitted that some people just do not like them). A telephone answering machine can also be useful if you are offering a phone-and-type service (see Chapter 9) or a telephone answering service.

The operation of the machine is very simple. You record a message on to a tape and when you connect the machine up this is played to callers automatically. Callers can be invited to leave a message which is recorded on another tape for you to listen to later.

Responding to the messages recorded on the machine is important. Make sure that you listen to the tape every day (or whenever you use it) and deal promptly with any messages. One disadvantage of a telephone answering machine is that many of your customers will ask you to call them back. And this means that *you* will have to pay for the phone call.

The simplest telephone answering machines can be purchased for £40 or less. You should be able to buy a more sophisticated model plus a telephone and by-pass monitor (which allows you to hear the caller before you decide to speak) ready to plug into your existing telephone socket for under £100.

Chapter 8
Daily Operation of the Business

Organising your time

Lack of organisation is one of the major time-wasters of any business. It is anathema to a home-based typing service. For you time *is* money. If you work inefficiently, are constantly interrupted, have to spend hours sorting out materials before you can begin an assignment, or find that your customers spend half the day at your house drinking coffee, you need to organise your time better!

When you first start your typing service you may encounter time management problems. Among them determining how much work you can deal with in a given time and keeping distractions (both personal and business) to a minimum, will probably rate quite highly.

Because running a home-based typing service is such a very personalised occupation, you will have to learn from your own experience how to estimate the time needed to complete assignments and how to minimise interruptions. However, you can save yourself a lot of stress and harassment if you keep a daily time chart. On this chart you should list your plans for the day and estimate how much time each job will take. At the end of the day, record how much time the job *actually* consumed, and include a note of all the additional unexpected tasks or distractions you had to contend with during the day and how long *they* took. After a few days of this you will probably find that you not only tend to underestimate the time required to accomplish typing assignments but that distractions and interruptions take up a considerable amount of your 'working' time and interfere with your planned work periods.

When you estimate the time needed to finish an assignment don't forget to include time spent with the customer *beforehand*, proof-reading, and time spent going over the completed work with the customer *afterwards*. Make an allowance for corrections or rewording and then add extra time for possible interruptions or distractions. It is better to risk overestimating the time required to complete a task (leaving you with extra time for emergencies, other tasks, or just enjoying yourself) than it is to live in a permanent frenzy of activity trying to meet impossible deadlines and resenting every interruption.

Go through your own time chart and find out where *you* are losing time. The following checklist will help you to pinpoint and eliminate the major time-consuming problems.

1. Procrastination

Inevitably there will be times when you are faced with an assignment that you know is going to be a chore and you find innumerable excuses to avoid starting it. We all procrastinate at times, and if you are working from home this can be a particularly difficult problem: it is all too easy to put off the dreaded assignment until the last minute. Deferring unpleasant tasks may mean that the work is rushed and perhaps badly done. If you find procrastination is often a problem you will need to tackle it positively. First, find out what sort of assignments you tend to defer. Do you hate typing tables, or envelopes, or do you find it difficult to make a start on a long thesis or manuscript? Make a particular effort to deal with those problem areas. If you hate typing tables, for example, and have a document that contains quite a few, try typing all the tables *first* while the tabs are set and you are fresh. Once they are done you will probably be able to get through the rest of the work in double-quick time. If you dread long and complex tasks then break them up into manageable chunks, plan a timetable for completion of each part and make yourself stick to it. In time you should be able to tackle any assignment with confidence and ease.

2. Callers

There are two types of caller who may disrupt your routine: personal callers (family, friends, the milkman, salesman etc) and unexpected customers. These interruptions break your concentration and take up valuable time. You will need to be particularly firm with the former. Tell them you're busy and ask them to call again at a more convenient time.

Unexpected customers are more difficult to deal with. How you tackle this will depend to some extent on how much work you have to do and whether you feel it necessary to tolerate 'drop-in' customers in order to maintain their goodwill. Unfortunately, there are some customers who tend to treat home-typists like doormats! They will turn up at weekends, at mealtimes and during the evening, never apologise for interrupting what is probably your leisure time, and expect you to drop everything in order to deal with their 'urgent' work. You may be happy to accept this sort of thing, especially in the initial stages while you are building up a work-load, but if you find it is a problem you will have to point out tactfully that it is in your customers' best interests to *telephone* you first for an appointment. They may have a wasted journey if you are out, for example. Give them one of your business cards so that they have a note of your phone number and write your business hours on the back for persistent offenders. It is much easier to explain to a customer that it is not convenient for them to call that evening if they are on the telephone than it is if they are standing on your doorstep!

3. Telephone calls

Look at your time chart. Do you make several telephone calls during the day all at different times? You can save yourself time and avoid 'losing the thread' of your work if you can group calls at a convenient break point. Plan each call in advance. Prepare a list of the points you want to make and, as you ask each question, write the answer next to it on the sheet. Be brief. Once you have the information you require, end the call. Don't get caught up in socialising.

If you are constantly interrupted by people phoning you, you might consider buying or hiring an answering machine. Some people dislike using these and you *may* lose custom if you are never available to answer the telephone personally, but they can be a boon if you have a long and complicated assignment to complete and are constantly having to break off to answer the telephone.

When making outgoing calls, use any time while 'on hold' (a long cord and shoulder rest are good for this) to do filing, clear your desk, and so on. Another useful device is a telephone with a memory and re-dial facility. These are no more expensive than an ordinary telephone (you can purchase one for less than £20). If you are trying to get a number that is engaged you simply press a button and the number will be re-dialled automatically for you. This can be surprisingly time-saving as you can get on with your typing while the number is dialled.

4. Underestimating the time required to complete a task

This is a *very* common problem, especially in the early stages. Not only will you become more proficient as time goes on, you will also learn better how to judge the time required to complete an assignment. Look at the reasons *why* the assignment took longer to complete than expected. Did you find you had to slow down or stop because you weren't sure how your customer wanted the work done? You can avoid this by going through the work carefully, with your customer beforehand. Did you have to stop to hunt for files or references? By assembling all the equipment, books, and papers you need for a particular assignment before you start you can eliminate time wasted due to disorganisation. Don't forget to clear your desk of everything else. Remember to allow extra time for typing lots of figures, tables, bibliographies etc, or for interpreting poor handwriting or specialised terminology. Were you plagued by interruptions? If you can't eliminate or reduce interruptions perhaps you could organise your schedule so that you are working on the complex assignments during the quietest period of your day and dealing with the less demanding tasks (envelope addressing, filing and so on) during your more 'disturbed' periods. Remember to allow plenty of time for proof-reading, corrections and unexpected disruptions.

5. Corrections and alterations

Are corrections and alterations taking up more time than they should? Find out where your problems arise. If you are making a lot of mistakes you are either working too fast or are not concentrating on the task in hand. Give yourself plenty of time to complete the assignment and try to concentrate on *one* task at a time. Above all, *finish* one task before starting another.

Perhaps you are a poor proof-reader. If you find that you often miss mistakes on your own proof-reading of the work perhaps you could ask a friend to check your typing while you read the original. It is better to correct any typing errors *before* you hand over to the customer for checking. It hardly gives a good impression of your service if you hand over work that contains numerous typing errors.

If you find that certain customers often return asking for extensive alterations perhaps you could suggest that you prepare an initial draft for them and type up the final version from that, after any corrections and alterations have been made. In any event, if you are asked to make extensive alterations or corrections that are the customer's fault, you should make an additional charge to cover the necessary time and materials.

6. Priorities

Once you have got into the habit of making a list of tasks for the day you should try to assign *priorities* to those tasks. Decide which are the most critical and do those *first*, then if you are delayed later on at least you will have completed the most important assignments. Always finish one task before starting on the next. You will waste time and fail to do justice to any assignment if you constantly jump from one task to another.

7. More time-saving tips

Plan to make all your purchases of new supplies at the same time and arrange to visit the various suppliers in the most economic (in terms of time) order. If you are likely to be delayed anywhere take some proof-reading with you. (You can also proof-read during 'holding' time on the telephone.)

Ensure that your office, or desk, is organised efficiently. Keep frequently used items in your top drawers and clear away items that are rarely used. Establish a good simple filing system and *use* it. File every day. Avoid having piles of disorganised paper lying around because you don't know where to put them.

Take your post straight to your desk when it arrives, open it, and decide on a plan of action for each item immediately. If writing replies, making phone calls, or dealing with extra work is necessary, make a note of these at appropriate places on your day's work-plan.

8. Time for yourself

Don't get so involved in your typing service that you neglect your private life. You are not trying to work efficiently and eliminate time-wasting only to cram in even more work.

Try not to be overtaken by the desire to make more and more money. Inevitably the 'pound signs' will light up in your eyes when a customer calls offering you work and it is *very* difficult to turn work away, even when you are fully booked. If your business is successful there will inevitably be occasions when you *have* to turn work away. Unless you are 'going all out' and are prepared to let your business grow and expand rapidly (*and* work 15 hours per day) you could easily be put off by taking on too much too soon. If you really want to work only eight hours a day and are already fully booked, think carefully about what you'll have to forgo if you take on extra assignments.

Dealing with customers

Handling customers, especially your first dozen or so, can be a traumatic experience for a new home-typist. Even if you have had a lot of practice in previous employment or have always found it easy to 'get on' with people in general, you may find your role more difficult when you become a self-employed home-worker. Some home-typists find it more difficult to adopt a businesslike manner with a customer sitting in their lounge, for example, than they would with a customer in an office or shop. Remember that your home is also your place of work and, although good relations with your customer may be beneficial, they are not guests but business associates. An excess of small talk will not only waste your time, it may give the impression that you are not terribly efficient or businesslike.

Surprisingly, perhaps, your customers may have a similar problem. If you were sitting behind a counter in a town centre agency they would have no trouble at all in explaining their needs and asking for information: sitting in *your* lounge, drinking *your* coffee, they may feel rather less assertive and sure of themselves. As in any business the variety of customers you will meet is endless. Some, and particularly *other* small-business owners, will already have very firm ideas about the layout, spacing, copies and format they require. You will be able to ascertain the needs of these customers quickly, easily and with the minimum of fuss. Others will have only the vaguest idea of what they want, what you can provide, or how much information you need. With such a customer you will need to be able to ask all the relevant questions, find out his or her precise needs and clearly explain how you can supply them.

Directing the conversation

In any dealings with customers you will need to balance a friendly, helpful, interested manner with a businesslike approach that tells them you've got work to do. Be friendly, but don't allow your customers to intrude on your time by spending too long in chat. If you do have this problem, which is surprisingly common, bring their attention back to the work in hand by recapping, saying something like, 'Well Mrs Smith, I'll have two copies of your report ready for you by 3.00 pm on Friday then. Could you leave me a note of your telephone number in case I need to contact you in the meantime?' At the same time pick up your customer's work and stand up: this will almost certainly motivate your customer to do the same. Once you got them on their feet walk over to the door and hold it open for them. It doesn't matter if they start chatting again at this point as they're on the way out anyway!

Customers who are side-tracked in the middle of discussing their requirements also need direction. This can be particularly difficult if your service includes an element of 'interviewing' as would be necessary for a comprehensive curriculum vitae service for example. In this case you will have to allow sufficient time (at least half-an-hour) for discussing layout and style, content and presentation, and for taking down all the relevant details you require. Remember that *you* must take the leading role. If your customer is side-tracked *you* should bring his attention back to the work in hand. Your customers will expect you to take the lead in asking questions and proffering information.

It is much easier for both you and your customer to adopt the appropriate 'roles' if you have a room or area set aside for use as your 'office'. It may also give your customers confidence if they can see where you do the work. It can be nerve-racking for a student, for example, to leave the only copy of his precious thesis with an unknown person who simply puts it on top of the TV and goes back to washing the dog.

Telephone queries

Customers will almost invariably make the initial contact with you by telephone. Unlike a town centre typing agency you will get very few new customers turning up unexpectedly at the door. You will therefore need to develop a polite and proficient telephone manner. Most customers will be telephoning several typists and agencies to compare prices, so you need to be able to present *your* service as the best, if not the cheapest, available. Don't simply give your charges and leave it at that. It takes only a few seconds to ask the customers what their typing needs are. Emphasise your ability to provide the particular service your caller is looking for: a fast turnaround, a guarantee of accuracy, free copies, correction of grammar and spelling, collection/delivery, or whatever, *before* you tell them what your charges are. Be helpful and positive. Perhaps you could offer to send them a sample or a leaflet outlining your service and charges. This gives you a good opportunity to 'get your foot in the door' with a potential customer, even if they don't use you on this occasion.

Keep your appointments book (a diary will do) and a 'work in hand' journal by the telephone so that you can decide on your ability to meet a commitment while you're speaking to the customer. You may lose custom if you give the impression that you aren't sure whether you can fit in a piece of work or not, or if you have to leave the customer waiting on the line while you rummage about trying to find your appointments book.

There will be occasions when a new potential customer calls with some urgent typing work when you are fully booked. To some extent you need to be guided by your own judgement under these circumstances. If the customer is a small businessperson who may well come to you regularly, you may wish to put in some extra time with a view to securing future custom; likewise, you may want to fit in a regular user in order to maintain his or her custom. On the other hand, the customer may require a large one-off typing assignment completed (such as a thesis) and/or you may find it impossible to fit in the work. If this is the case don't simply tell the caller that you cannot do the work: apologise and explain that you are fully booked at that time, offer to send a leaflet outlining your service and charges for future use, and if possible provide the caller with another contact (perhaps another home-typist you know) who may be able to help. Hopefully, your caller will be impressed enough either to try you again in the future or to pass on your name to some other potential customer.

Dealing with several customers at once

During your working day you will also have customers calling at your home to collect or deliver work. For most of these you will have made an appointment, but many customers (especially regulars) will call without telephoning in advance. The fact that your customers may fail to keep an agreed appointment or may call on spec means that you will, on some occasions, have several customers on your premises at once. This should not be a problem as long as you can keep the customer you are dealing with at that time separate from the others. Many customers expect – even require – a degree of confidentiality in their dealings with you and may not be too happy if they have to discuss their requirements or check work in the presence of others.

Here again, a separate office in which you can go over the work with customers is the best situation. You can then leave unexpected callers in the comfort of your lounge while you attend to each caller individually in your interview area.

Ascertaining the customers' needs

One of your major aims when dealing with customers will be to find out what they want done and provide them with information about deadlines, charges, corrections, alterations and so on.

When your customer brings you an assignment, take time to go through it carefully with him *while he is there*. Make sure you ask about the kind of paper required, line spacing, margins, whether paragraphs should be indented, how the work should be laid out. Do customers want a particular type style? Do they want carbon copies/photocopies, and how many? Do they want you to produce a draft first for checking? Also, make sure you get a telephone number where you can contact them if need be. Obviously you don't want to ring unnecessarily, but you *may* have to.

If there are insertions and alterations are these clearly marked? Any insertions should (preferably) be marked 1, 2, 3, and so forth, in a bold colour with an arrow showing where in the text they are to be typed. The text to be inserted should be appropriately numbered and written on a separate sheet. Deletions should be crossed out with a single clear line. Any supplementary information about layout, paragraphing and so on should be written in a different coloured ink from the actual text – although it is, of course, easier for you if the only writing on a page is that which you have to type! Unfortunately, you will receive many badly written texts covered with unintelligible corrections and deletions and with little notes (to you) written all over them. If you are presented with an extensive document which has been substantially altered without any consistency you could offer to prepare an initial draft (for an extra charge, of course) which can then be used as a basis for any further alteration.

Bad handwriting

Perhaps the biggest bugbear of the home-typist is bad handwriting. Unless the writing is really terrible (and what is especially annoying, inconsistent) you should be able to understand it as long as the sentences are grammatically correct and of a non-technical nature. However, make sure that customers with poor handwriting print out personal names, place names and all technical, scientific and medical words clearly (preferably above the handwritten word). Don't be afraid to say that the handwriting is difficult to understand if it is. Most people already know if their handwriting is awful and won't be offended. If you think the handwriting or presentation is likely to slow you down, tell your customer in advance that your charge may be slightly higher because the work may take longer than normal to complete. Don't shock your customer by asking for substantially more than was expected when he or she comes to collect the work.

Remembering the customers' instructions

While you are going through the work with the customers make sure you attend to what they are saying. Don't be reading the bottom of the page if they are explaining something at the top. Most important of all, make a note of the customers' instructions immediately. Don't put it off until later. When you have several different assignments going at the same time it is all too easy to forget whether customer A wanted three copies on 80 g/m² white or whether customer B asked you to print addresses at the bottom of letters.

It is an excellent idea to have a set of pre-printed forms available for completion while you are interviewing the customer. You can type one of these yourself and have 50 or so photocopies produced. If you have a word processor, save a copy of the form on disc and run off batches as and when you need them. These should have details of the customer's name, address and telephone number(s) together with a summary of the work, any special requirements, the agreed deadline, charging policy adopted and the estimated cost. An example is shown on page 101. You can adapt this idea to suit your own requirements.

A properly completed form is not only an indispensable reference to remind you of the customer's requirements, it can be usefully integrated into your record-keeping system. The form can be filed in your 'work in hand' file initially, affixed to the appropriate invoice when the work is completed, and the whole lot attached to your copy receipt when the job has been paid for. You can transfer details to your cash book directly from the form.

Another advantage of such a form is that you retain full details of the work you have done for a customer. This can be extremely useful when that customer calls to request further work because you will have a note of your previous charging policy, how quickly the customer paid, whether the work took longer than expected, and so on.

Alterations, corrections and mistakes

However good a typist you are, you will on occasion make mistakes. There will also be times when you will be asked to make alterations because your *customer* has made a mistake or has decided to reword something. Alterations are endemic to some assignments. Masters' and doctoral theses, for example, normally have to be retyped at least once after submission for preliminary checking. If you have a word processor this is no problem as the

Typing service work-form

Customer's Details: Name ....

Address ....

....

Telephone (Home) ....

(Work) ....

Details of Work Required:

....

....

....

No of copies: ....   Type of copy: ....

Element type: ....   Spacing: ....

Margins: ....   Indentation: ....

Headings: ....   Paper: ....

Special Requirements: ....

....

Collection date and time: ....

Estimate cost: £...................   Actual cost: £...................

Copies: £...................

Postage: £...................

. Phone calls: £...................

Alterations: £...................

Others: £...................

TOTAL   £...................

Invoice No: ....   Receipt No: ....

Notes:

bulk of the already stored text will remain the same; you will only have to retype and insert the alterations. Using a conventional typewriter you will have to retype the whole lot. This can be a very long job – such theses usually being somewhere between 10,000 and 80,000 words long – so you should charge accordingly.

Charging for changes

One of the most frequently asked questions is 'Should I charge for corrections?' A reasonable policy to adopt is that if a mistake is *yours*, correct it free of charge; if a mistake is the *customer's*, charge him.

Charging customers for mistakes can be problematical if you don't charge an hourly rate. The simplest approach is probably to go through the alterations with the customer, explain that you will have to charge for them and then give a reasonable estimated price. This approach is usually most acceptable to the customer.

Who is to blame?

Problems can arise when the customer feels that he or she *has* given you the correct instructions or whatever, but you have interpreted them wrongly. This is to be avoided at all costs! Careful notes on your work-generation form should help but occasionally customers do not fully understand *what* the typist means by 'indentation', 'block paragraphs', 'bold type', '10 pitch', and so on, and are unpleasantly surprised by the appearance of the finished product.

Samples showing a variety of type styles and formats as well as the various acceptable methods of punctuation, page continuation, numbering and so on, can eliminate this problem. It is rarely a good idea to allow a customer to say 'Oh, you lay it out the way you think it should be' or 'You're the expert, I'll leave that to you.' When they see the finished product they may change their minds! If you are asked for advice about layout, punctuation etc, by all means give it. That is, after all, part of your service. But make sure the customer understands exactly *how* you intend to present the work. Show samples to clarify your proposals and ensure that your customer agrees with these.

Making alterations

Changes are no problem if you have a word processor, but you will otherwise have to run off an entire new page if you have made even a small mistake on it and this can, on occasion, be a disadvantage.

Experienced typists usually know that they have made a mistake as soon as they do it. The best policy is to make correction immediately. If you leave it till the end of the page or, worse, till the end of the assignment, you may have difficulty lining up the paper exactly and the correction may look rather messy. You will always make immediate corrections (assuming you spot them) when you are using a word processor or electronic typewriter, of course.

Correction ribbons
Of the various conventional correction methods, a typewriter fitted with a correction ribbon undoubtedly produces the most acceptable result. Unfortunately, this method does have drawbacks. In the first place, a correction ribbon will only work with the expensive, use-once film ribbons and not with fabric ribbons. In addition, if you fail to spot the mistake straight away and carry on typing further down the page it can be difficult to line up the mistake exactly (the key must hit the paper in the same place as before to lift off the incorrect letter(s)). It is even more difficult if you miss the mistake entirely and take the page out of the machine. Another problem is that any carbon copies are *not* corrected. You will still have to correct these separately using a typewriter rubber or correction fluid.

Rubbing out
If you don't have a correction ribbon you will have to make corrections using either a typewriter rubber, correction fluid or correction paper. Typewriter rubbers are either round and flat or else in pencil form. Pencil-type erasers can be more precisely manipulated (you only rub out the bit you want to rub out!), they can be sharpened to maintain a clean, well angled surface, and usually incorporate a rubber-dust brush on the other end: useful for brushing residual dust off the paper prior to retyping. The major problems with rub-out corrections include (a) the difficulty of achieving a neat correction on some types of paper, (b) the possibility of smudging, rubbing a hole in the paper, and restricting the correction to a small area, and (c) the fact that rubber dust can fall into the machine, clogging up the works. In principle, the last problem should never arise because rub-out corrections should always be made with the carriage extended over the desk so that rubber-dust falls on to the desk rather than into the typewriter. However, in practice, many typists are in the habit of making such corrections over the key-nest. Don't do this to your machine. The time spent moving the carriage to one side will

more than compensate for the extra maintenance you would otherwise have to put into keeping your machine running smoothly.

An erasing shield (a piece of plastic or card with a number of shaped holes cut in it) can be useful for rub-out corrections. You simply place an appropriately shaped hole in the shield over the offending text and rub out inside the hole. It can be difficult to use while the paper is still in the machine.

Correction fluids and papers

These days rub-out corrections seem rather old-fashioned compared with correction fluid/paper corrections. However a properly executed rub-out correction should be barely noticeable, whereas a badly executed fluid correction will look horrendous! Correction fluid/paper can be a quick and convenient way of making corrections and, used properly, is usually acceptable to customers.

Correction paper works on the principle of disguising the offensive letter(s) with a coat of white dust and typing the correction over this. You backspace to the mistake, insert the correction paper between the page and the ribbon, retype the error, remove the correction paper, backspace again and type in the correct letter(s). This is quicker than either rubbing out or using correction fluid but has the disadvantage that the white powder tends to rub or wear off with time leaving the error showing through under the correction. In addition, you will not have a 'clean' correction unless you use a part of the correction paper that has *not* been used before.

Used properly, correction fluid can produce a very neat correction. It is a particularly useful method when producing an original which will subsequently be photocopied, as a fluid correction will not show on the photocopies (and is barely perceptible on the original) whereas a paper correction or rub-out may produce a shadow. Correction fluid (such as Tipp-Ex, Snopake and Liquid Paper) can be obtained in a variety of colours for use on coloured papers. It comes in a small bottle with an applicator brush. Corrections can be made with the paper in or out of the typewriter by carefully spreading a small amount of the fluid over the mistake, waiting for it to dry completely (this usually takes only a few seconds) then retyping the correct letter(s) on top of the dried fluid. Messy corrections will be made if the fluid is too thick (thinning fluids are available for diluting correcting fluid that has become too dry), or if the fluid is not allowed to dry completely before the correction is made. It is normally easier, and gives a better finished appearance, if a whole word is obliterated and retyped rather than just the incorrect letter(s). By the way, if you inadvertently get correcting fluid on the keys, paper guide markings or platen, you can remove this with a small amount of thinning fluid on a piece of soft cloth.

Proof-reading

Careful proof-reading is essential, possibly even more important than accurate typing. It can mean the difference between handing over a piece of work that is full of glaring errors and silly mistakes and providing a letter-perfect product.

It is better to have a time gap between typing and proof-reading, as it can be remarkably difficult to spot your own typing errors shortly after you've finished a piece of work.

For longer papers or those with a lot of numbers you will find proof-reading easier if you can get someone to read the typed copy while you read the original out loud. If you are a fast reader, you may find accurate proof-reading particularly difficult because you will have been reading groups of words at a glance. For good proof-reading you need to re-train yourself to read individual *letters* in the words. Make a conscious effort to slow yourself down. If you find yourself running ahead, use a ruler or piece of paper with a slot cut in it to fix your attention on one line or group of words at a time.

When you find a mistake, either correct it immediately or make a pencilled note of the error in the margin and make the correction later.

If you have a word-processor, a spelling check program will substantially reduce the time spent proof-reading as misspelled words will be picked up for you. However, a spell-checker will *not* pick up errors where an inappropriate but correctly spelled word is inserted or where you have missed out, transposed, or duplicated portions of text. For example, 'James was hear' would not be detected as incorrect. Neither would grammatical gobbledegook such as 'He went then can we have three copies!'

Common errors

Apart from simple spelling mistakes and errors involving the substitution of one correctly spelled word for another ('there' for 'their') common typing errors include missing out chunks of text, repeating double letters, missing out letters in a word (especially in long words), breaks in continuity between one page and the next, repeating or missing out words, faulty punctuation and errors in typing numbers.

It is particularly easy to omit a section or paragraph especially if it starts with the same word or phrase as the next. Repeating letters, as in the words 'confidentialiity' and 'controllling' is another common error, difficult to detect. Beware of other hard-to-spot mistakes such as typing 'affect' for 'effect' (or vice versa), transposing letters (for example typing 'reciept' for 'receipt', or missing letters out (for example typing 'satelite' instead of 'satellite') Possibly the most easily overlooked errors lie in small words, with only one letter difference, such as it/is/in/if, or/on, as/at and so on.

Certain words have alternative forms of spelling (equally correct) but your customer may have a preference. Find out what it is and be consistent. Examples are:

realise/realize (-ise or -ize ending)   grey/gray
adviser/advisor   despatch/dispatch
medieval/mediaeval   carcass/carcase

Seasonal flexibility – go with your customers

When you first start your typing service you may want to take on *any* kind of typing you can get. This is a good way to find out what market there is in your area: something that is often difficult to predict in advance.

Adopting a flexible approach is probably essential in the early stages. Even if you ultimately intend to specialise you will almost certainly need to diversify initially. A specialist service usually takes time to build up. Your eventual goal, for instance, may be to work exclusively for a number of small businesses in the area. There is nothing wrong with this idea: once you have an established network of customers your advertising costs will be low, you will 'know' your customers, and the work should be predictable and, hopefully, fairly regular. However, you won't achieve a full work-load of this sort immediately. It may take up to a year of continual advertising and regular mail shots to attract a sufficient, suitable, work supply.

There are disadvantages in specialising. If you work almost exclusively for a few established customers, for example, it can be very difficult to take holidays, reduce or increase your work-load for any reason or avoid periods of over and under work.

Consider the following example. Your service is geared to the secretarial work of ten small businesses and you also take seasonal overflow work from two large organisations. One of the big firms phones you because they have 1000 invoices to be typed by the following week. Since you are in a slack period generally you agree to take them. Later that day two of your small firms phone to ask you to prepare 20 letters and a 200-page bill of quantities. (You cannot refuse either since they both have retainer contracts with you.) The following day another two of your small businesses want you to type 300 envelopes and 15 sets of accounts respectively. You suddenly find yourself working from 6.00 am to 11.00 pm every day!

This won't always happen, of course. Most of the time you will probably have a regular, steady, supply of work. The point is, if you have this kind of arrangement you may forgo control over how much, how little, or what you do. So think about the disadvantages as well as the advantages of such a situation.

You can often maintain greater flexibility, and will certainly have to deal with a broader variety of people and assignments, if you retain an open approach. The disadvantages of flexibility are that your work-load may be more irregular, you will probably have to advertise more widely and frequently, you will have to deal with more new customers, you will need a wider range of skills and you may suffer from more bad debts.

On the other hand, you will have little difficulty in turning work away when it suits you, taking holidays and expanding or reducing your work-load as you wish. You will also have the intellectual satisfaction and stimulation of dealing with a great variety of assignments and meeting lots of new people.

For the many home-typists who adopt the flexible approach their work-load often has a seasonal variability. The bulk of dissertations and theses, for example, will come to the end of the college or university term; large organisations often have to get out special Christmas promotions and bulk mailings in December; accountants are usually swamped with tax computations, accounts and tax returns during March and April, and so on.

During these peak periods you are likely to be overrun with work: in fact you may wish to take on temporary staff (see Chapter 12), but at other times you will need to ensure that you have sufficient non-seasonal work to keep you going.

You will need to gear your advertising appropriately not only to capture the 'peak' markets, but also to have a good supply of customers waiting in the wings during your infill periods. Don't wait until you run out of work to start advertising for more. Plan well in advance. About a fortnight before you think one of your seasonal 'flushes' will end, you should be advertising for your next batch of customers. You will learn from experience what type of promotion achieves the best results for you.

By following the requirements of your local customers your typing service will be able to develop and grow to its full potential, *you* will remain in charge of what you do and when you do it, and you will be able to maintain and develop an immense range of skills which will stand you in good stead for the future.

Daily money matters

Cash or cheque

Money will flow through your business via your petty cash box and your business bank account. You can, of course, use a personal bank account for business receipts and payments but, as noted in Chapter 4, this *may* cause problems if you need to prove the state of your business banking for tax purposes.

Keep a good supply of change in your petty cash box. This will be useful for small purchases and particularly necessary when you need to give change to customers. A £20 float should suffice.

For relatively small jobs your customers will probably pay in cash, but they may want to pay by cheque for larger, more expensive, assignments. Accepting a cheque imposes some risk on you but you can minimise this by following these guideliness:

1. Only accept a personal cheque if the customer has a cheque guarantee card to support it. Even students can normally get these from their banks. Otherwise insist on cash.
2. Check the following details on the cheque: the date, your name (or business name if you have a separate account); the words and figures agree; the cheque has been signed (in your presence).
3. Check the following details on the card: the expiry date (it should not have run out); the signature matches the one on the cheque; the *code* numbers on the card and cheque are the same (the code number is *not* the card number).
4. Ensure that the cheque is for £50 or under. If the bill is over this amount, ask your customer to give you more than one cheque (all £50 or less) or the balance in cash, and make out an invoice for each cheque. Your customers may object to this if they have to pay bank charges for each cheque issued.

but a cheque guarantee card normally only 'guarantees' a cheque up to £50: above this amount the bank may refuse to honour the cheque if their client has insufficient funds in his or her account.

5. Most cheque cards have the account holder's name printed on them. Make sure this *is* your customer's name. If in any doubt ask to see some further identification such as driver's licence, passport, child benefit or pension book.

6. Write the card number (not the code number) on the back of the cheque.

7. Ensure you have the customer's correct name and address in case of any query. (You should already have this if you fully completed one of your work forms at the outset.)

8. Pay cheques in as soon as possible.

Credit cards

An alternative to accepting payment by either cash or cheque is to offer a credit card facility. You *must* have a separate business bank account and need to hire (or buy) an imprinting machine. The credit card companies provides the sales slips. You simply bank your copies of these slips and, at the end of the month, the credit card company totals your sales for the month and charges you a small percentage for providing the service. (This charge should be built into your quotations.)

The advantage of accepting credit cards for payment is that provided the card hasn't expired, isn't defaced, and isn't on your list of stolen cards (issued by your bank), you can't be held liable for bad debts. It is up to the credit card company to get the money from the customer; you will already have been paid. Ask your bank for further information on this facility.

When should the customer pay?

When the customer pays for your service will depend upon (a) the type and cost of the job, (b) the status of the customer, and (c) the agreement between you.

For small one-off jobs, such as the production of a few letters, you should expect payment upon the customer's receipt or collection of the finished work. Give customers time to go through the typing on your premises so that they are satisfied that it is correct before being asked for payment.

If you are working substantially on a postal system you will either have to adopt a policy of asking for a deposit (or full payment) in advance, or invoice customers when you return the finished product to them. If you elect to invoice customers, state your terms on the invoice (please pay immediately, 30 days net, or whatever).

Typists who work regularly for business customers may have a quarterly retaining fee system and then invoice the client for any work done separately (probably monthly). You will send out your quarterly retaining fee invoice every three months (about a month before it is due for renewal) and other invoices on a regular basis. Large organisations may have a long and complicated payment procedure, but if you have to wait longer than 28 days, send out a reminder and phone the client to find out why you have not been paid.

It is generally better (and normally expected) that 'personal' customers, such as writers, students and job-seekers, should pay *immediately* upon receipt of the finished work. Unless your customer is a regular user of your service, or you are otherwise *certain* you will be paid, it is rarely a good idea to give credit to personal customers. If your customers arrive and 'suddenly' find they can't pay you on the spot, it would be quite reasonable to refuse to let them take the work away, especially if it is an expensive job. Explain that it is your policy to retain the work until payment is made and suggest they arrange to call again later with the money and collect the work then.

Occasionally, you will do an extensive piece of work for a personal customer that cannot reasonably be checked 'on the spot' (a book or play script, for example). If the customer wants to take the work away for checking and is concerned about paying you the full amount before the work is checked, ask for a substantial deposit and only allow the customer to take one copy away. You should also ask for identification to confirm the customer's name and address in case of future difficulties. Make definite arrangements for the collection of further copies/payment of outstanding sum and confirm your correction/alteration policy with the customer before he or she leaves.

Some services, especially personal postal ones, such as the preparation and production of a CV, are normally paid for in advance. If you charge customers in advance for such a service, make sure you explain that money will be refunded if the customer is dissatisfied and *returns everything to you within a certain period of time* (normally within a fortnight or ten days). You might also like to ask for an advance deposit on a very large job, especially if it is for a new customer.

Paying your creditors

Most of your day-to-day purchases will be on a cash basis. That is, you will pay for the goods (stamps, paperclips, erasers etc) and services (photocopying, printing) as soon as you buy them. Once you are established you may be able to set up credit arrangements with your major suppliers who will then invoice you for the purchases. This is obviously better for *you* because you don't have to take money out of your business until later.

If you have several creditors and lessors you should have a properly organised system of payment which ensures that you neither pay unnecessarily early, nor invariably put off payments until you receive the final demand. Not only do you want to retain the goodwill of your creditors, you should not subject them to the nuisances you yourself are trying to avoid.

Check the financial state of your typing service *regularly*, not just when the annual accounts are prepared. Make sure you have sufficient funds to pay your creditors (even if you don't *actually* pay them until later). Are you *owed* more money by debtors than *you* owe to creditors? What would happen to your service if your debtors decided not to pay you? Would you still be solvent? Once you are dealing with invoiced customers and are paying for your supplies on credit you need to be especially careful about watching your cash flow. Things can easily get out of hand.

A checklist to make your typing service run smoothly

- Keep a daily work chart to find out where you are losing or wasting time. Once you have isolated your problem areas take positive action to eliminate or reduce them.
- Assign priorities to your work and always complete one task before beginning another.
- Allow plenty of time to complete an assignment. Remember to allow for proof-reading, corrections and interruptions.
- Do not postpone important matters that are unpleasant. They will block your brain and reduce your creativity and working capacity. Do the unpleasant things first, then the rest of the day is easy.
- Don't allow family and friends to intrude on your working time.
- Group telephone calls. Plan calls in advance. Separate *chat* from information. Keep an egg-timer by the phone. Get an

answering machine if you are constantly interrupted by telephone calls.

- Don't take on more work than you can handle.
- Compile a list of other typists who can help with seasonal overloads.
- Prepare a set of work generation forms tailored to your own service and requirements.
- File daily. Deal with post straight away.
- Keep your desk clear of everything but the assignment in hand.
- Set up a contact and customer file (an address book or index cards will do) detailing names, addresses and telephone numbers of your clients and contacts.
- Change typewriter ribbons after every 20–25 pages of text. Check the last page typed against the *first* page typed to see if it's time to change. Keep old ribbons for drafts and unimportant jobs.
- Proof-read carefully. Use a ruler or guide to focus your attention, or read aloud to another person.
- Always get a telephone number where you can contact your customer if you run into difficulties. Let the customer know as soon as possible if you cannot meet a deadline.
- Advertise well in advance of your need for more work.
- Go through the work *carefully* with new customers before they leave. Make sure that *you* understand their requirements and that *they* are aware of your pricing/alteration/correction policies.
- Make time to go through your records regularly (once a month when you total your cash book is a good time). Is your service doing as well as you predicted? Are you having any problems with debtors/creditors?
- Above all *enjoy* your typing service. You will not do your business justice if you are doing it half-heartedly or find the pressures difficult to cope with. Put *yourself* in your daily schedule.

Chapter 9

Typing Plus: Offering Additional Services

Running a home-typing service doesn't necessarily mean restricting yourself to copy typing at home. There is an almost endless range of additional services you can offer which will enhance and improve your business. Some of these, such as photocopying and audio-typing, have already been covered in Chapter 7. Other supplementary services you might like to consider are:

Photocopying

As well as relieving you of the need to make carbon copies, photocopying can be offered as a separate facility to your customers. A great many people need to have photocopies made whether or not they also require typing and, provided your location is convenient and your rates are reasonable, you should be able to attract customers purely on the basis of a photocopying service.

Collection and delivery

This is one of the commonest extras offered by home-typists and for good reason. Unless you live in the centre of a town or on a major road you are likely to be somewhat out of the way for your customers. Provided your service is of a high quality and your rates are reasonable this is not likely to be a severe hindrance. However, you will undoubtedly broaden the range of potential customers if you can offer to collect work and deliver it at their convenience.

This service can be especially useful for other small businesses who often do not have the *time* to travel to and from a secretarial agency delivering and collecting typing.

Apart from enhancing your service in the eyes of your customers, collection and delivery has other advantages. You can reduce the number of drop-in customers and have more control over how long you spend chatting to them. (It is easier to finalise dealings if *you* have to leave *their* premises than if you have to extricate them from yours!) On the other hand, the time you spend travelling uses fuel (or pedal power) and takes up *your* time. You are not at home to take telephone calls from potential customers or to carry on with other assignments.

You will have to make a financial assessment of the cost of providing the service. Allow for petrol, wear and tear on the car, and your travelling time. For short runs you may simply want to include the cost of collection and delivery in the price of the work, but make a charge for longer (or frequent) journeys. Whether you are providing a free service to attract custom or whether you are making a charge (either at cost or for a profit) for it, you should know how much the service is actually costing *you*. Remember to allow for these costs in your annual accounts and in your day-to-day cash flow and forecasting.

'Mobile' secretary

Providing a mobile secretarial service is quite different from working at home. Apart from slightly different equipment needs (you will need a *portable* electric typewriter or word processor, a telephone and a car), you will be working predominantly in other people's premises, probably using their stationery and doing a wider range of secretarial jobs (filing, drafting letters, taking shorthand, making bookings, bookkeeping and so on) than you would working from home. You will almost certainly want to charge by the hour for a service of this kind. Your charges will need to take into account travelling costs, any materials you have to provide, and wear and tear on your portable equipment. Some of your costs may be lower because you will be using your customers' heat, light, electricity and premises.

This kind of service is relatively rare although there *is* a demand for it. In rural areas, farmers and landowners may be delighted to have someone to do the office work once a week. They certainly won't have the time to bring the work to you and there are innumerable businesses with insufficient secretarial needs to employ staff, even on a part-time basis. The harassed owners of such concerns will often be very pleased to have a professional secretary calling once a week or so to type letters, keep filing up to date, do the bookkeeping, and so forth. Larger organisations with seasonal overloads (or occasional needs for fill-in staff due to sickness or holidays) may also take you on as an occasional freelance part-timer – especially as your rates are likely to be considerably less than those of the town centre agencies.

The major problem with this kind of service is attracting sufficient custom. Mail shots, directed personally to the most likely businesses in your area, together with a series of bold newspaper advertisements, will probably reap the best rewards. But you will need to stick at it and sell yourself! Small businesses that have struggled on for years without clerical staff may not realise what a benefit your service could be. Larger organisations, used to dealing with town centre agencies, may be dubious about taking on a freelance. In both cases your advertising will have to convince the customer that you know what you are doing. Follow up your mail shot with telephone calls: if possible, ask if you can call personally to discuss your service and how it can enhance/improve the quality (and therefore, by implication, the profits) of the business concerned.

Bookkeeping

Looming large in the problems encountered by many small businesses is the need to keep proper records. Bookkeeping, either at the client's premises or your own, is a valuable and much demanded skill in its own right. Combine it with a good range of secretarial abilities and you are on to a real winner.

If your bookkeeping skills are rusty (or non-existent) there are classes at colleges of further education and adult education establishments which will bring you up to peak form. It is also possible to learn bookkeeping and basic accounting by correspondence course. This is often a very good method of learning the basics because you can take the course at your own pace and in your own time.

Another possibility, and one that is fairly popular among home-typist partnerships, is to join forces with someone who already has good bookkeeping skills but lacks typing ability. If you don't want to go into full partnership, it is possible to combine *some* of your mutual needs (such as advertising a bookkeeping/typing service simultaneously and thus reducing the costs of *both* members), while retaining independence when it comes to actually doing the work and taking the profits. One of you takes the bookkeeping, the other takes the typing, and you invoice the customer separately. You can also usefully pass on work to each other: many business users of a typing service also have occasional bookkeeping needs and vice versa. You will also have someone to do *your* books, perhaps in return for some typing or printing!

Telephone answering

Again, there are a lot of small businesses who could use a telephone answering service: doctors, plumbers, electricians, salesmen, in fact anyone who is usually on the move and therefore not available to take telephone calls. You can charge customers a quarterly fee plus a small additional sum determined by the number of calls received for them. Some telephone answering services charge a flat weekly rate (£3.00 to £10.00 per week being typical).

A number of companies also advertise for people to provide a telephone answering service. These companies more often than not want you to act as their agent – either passing on contacts to them, or actually dealing with them yourself (they may want to leave samples on your premises; check the implications with your insurance company before agreeing). You may be offered a commission on sales rather than a set fee or weekly rate, so make sure you know what you're letting yourself in for if you take on something like this.

A well organised telephone answering service can make a small profit if properly run but it does have a number of drawbacks. First, you will have to stay in the house for most of the day, every day. This may be ideal if you are virtually housebound but can be quite a strain if you are normally able to get out and about. (You won't even be able to go out to buy more typing paper unless you can get someone else to cover for you while you're gone.) Second, if you have a lot of telephone calls for your clients, you may be losing custom for your typing service because your *own* customers cannot get through. In addition, your service may be badly affected if your telephone is out of order for any reason. Unlike faults with your typing equipment, getting a telephone line repaired is out of your hands and can take quite some time, although priority is usually given to business lines. One freelance accountant lost a considerable amount of business when his telephone line was out of order during a telephone engineer's strike – he had to wait ten weeks to have it restored. Perhaps the biggest problem of all is that the phone may never stop ringing! This is fine if you can cope with it, but it will interfere considerably with your typing output.

Phone and type

This sort of secretarial service is popular with firms of decorators, plumbers, electricians, builders and suchlike, but takes quite a long time to establish.

Basically, you offer to be available during certain hours to take phone calls from your customers who will provide details over the phone of estimates, invoices, letters and so on. You then type this – often on to your customers' own headed paper – mail the correspondence direct and keep a copy for your customer. This is particularly useful for businessmen on the move who want correspondence dealt with quickly. One typist, for example, had an arrangement whereby a firm of decorators would visit their client and make an estimate of the cost of doing the required decoration; they would phone the details through to the typist who would prepare a very professional estimate on their headed paper and post it the same day to the decorators' client.

Although the ability to take shorthand is not absolutely essential for this kind of service it will be a great aid and you should consider taking a course, or teaching yourself, if you do not already have this skill.

Apart from the fact that you have to be available to take calls from your customers (or provide an answering machine), the major problem with a service like this is that it often takes quite a long time to build up. As well as being able to convince potential users that *their* business will be greatly improved by using your service, you may well have to spend some time gaining their trust, especially if you will be signing letters and posting them direct.

Computer services

This must be one of the cheapest, easiest and most versatile of office services you can run from home. Personal computers are relatively cheap and offer a multitude of business applications with which you can tempt customers. Not only can a personal computer (with a printer) be used as a word processor, it can also be modified to deal with telex, teletex and electronic mail (see next section). You can also offer a comprehensive range of office services which might be of particular interest to small businesses, such as the maintenance of staff records, wages preparation, bookkeeping and accounts, cash flow forecasting, stock control, invoicing, storage of information and records of all kinds.

However, the Data Protection Act requires any business that

117

holds personal information on individuals (and this includes names and addresses) on *computer* files to register with the Data Protection Registrar, Springfield House, Water Lane, Wilmslow, Cheshire SK9 5AX (telephone 0625 535777 for enquiries).

In addition to general business programs such as those described above (which retail for between £10 and £40) you can also get programs that are specifically aimed at certain types of small business, such as hoteliers, video rental shops, estate agents, and so on. These are more expensive (£50 upwards) but are more closely matched to the requirements of one particular type of business. If you have clients who want you to take over and computerise the administration of their business they may be prepared to pay for a specific computer program and then pay you a monthly or quarterly fee for operating it. If you are a whizz with a computer you can do your own programming, producing software tailor-made to your customers' requirements.

Be very careful if you do decide to take over the affairs of a business in this way. You will need to be especially scrupulous about confidentiality and should ensure that you keep at least two copies of the information relevant to that business in case you damage or accidentally erase one copy.

The best way to find out about computers, what they can do and how they do it, is to go out and try some out! If you are totally inexperienced you could get some hands-on experience by taking one of the multitude of computer experience courses that are available, or failing that, ask a knowledgeable friend to let you practise on his or her computer. The frequent computer/word-processor shows that are held in most large towns are another source of ideas and information though these are usually so crowded you will probably not get a chance to practise much.

Many word processors can actually be used like computers and can often be used with a range of business software. The Amstrad PCW 8256, for example, now has an extensive range of business software. Other companies are now following Amstrad's lead and the personal computer/word-processor market is expanding rapidly so you will need to undertake your own research in order to get the best deal when you buy.

One other point you might like to consider is that, as well as providing a service for your customers, business software would be useful for running your *own* service too. You can produce invoices, statements, annual accounts, maintain sales and purchase ledgers and cash book, keep a directory of customers, produce financial forecasts and so on simply by pressing a few keys.

Electronic communications services

If you really want to branch out you might like to consider offering telex, teletex or other electronic mail services to local businesses which lack these facilities. Advances in computer communications technology mean that you can now link up a personal computer, word processor and even some electronic typewriters, to the telephone network and use these services at a fraction of the cost of using dedicated equipment (such as the 'old' telex machines).

As well as a computer/word processor you will need a modem which converts the signals produced by your computer into a form that can be sent down a telephone line; a suitable interface to convert parallel signals into series signals (your computer may have one built in); a telephone socket (essential for some modems); and a program that will allow your computer to work as part of a network (this is normally supplied with the modem). Your local computer supplier will be able to advise you on the requirements of your system. You can obtain a complete package (modem, interface, software and network subscription) for around £100–£200.

What you can do with the system will depend on which networks you join. There are two broad categories of use: electronic mail and viewdata.

Electronic mail

Several major communications companies are now offering public electronic mail systems: Telecom Gold, Easylink and One-to-One are examples. When a subscriber to one of these services wants to contact another, he uses his own computer or word processor to formulate the message and establish a telephone link with the system supplier's computer. This computer holds the 'mailboxes' of all the subscribers, allowing messages to be left in one or more specific subscribers' mailboxes (see page 120). The message is stored until the recipient chooses to 'interrogate' his mailbox and extract it, either in text form on a VDU or as hard copy via the printer.

Annual subscription, monthly mailbox rental, on-line and storage charges vary among suppliers. That, compounded by the fact that this is one of the most rapidly developing areas in communications technology at the present time, means that you will need to carry out your own needs/costs analysis to find out the most appropriate system for your service. Remember to include the cost of telephone calls and rental. The numerous monthly

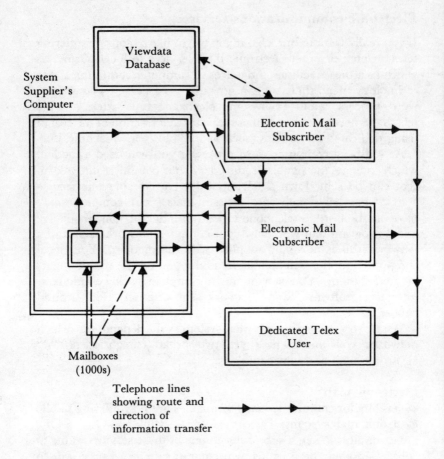

System
Supplier's
Computer

Mailboxes
(1000s)

Telephone lines
showing route and
direction of
information transfer

Electronic Mail Network

computing magazines and the annual *Daily Mail Home Computing Guide* provide abundant up-to-date information about the costs, availability and uses of electronic mail facilities.

In general, electronic mail is a much cheaper way of sending written (text) information than traditional telex or even ordinary postage. The cost of transmitting ten pages of text is only about 5p, for example, cheaper even than the cost of a stamp. In addition, the equipment and ongoing costs are usually lower, adding to its appeal.

Electronic telex and teletex

Telex is basically a teleprinter service using the public telephone system. A dedicated desk-top telex (such as the 3M Whisper

Telex) retails for about £1200. Line rental is currently £90 per quarter and you also pay for the time you use transmitting information. In addition, if you are going to receive messages for your customers, you must leave your teleprinter switched on all day and night.

Teletex (also known as super-telex) seems set to take over from telex as the major text communication method. Essentially, it is the same as the public electronic mail system: it provides ordinary word processors and computers with links to the telex network. It is considerably cheaper both in terms of equipment required and ongoing costs than traditional telex. Some electronic mail suppliers include a telex 'gateway' facility for a marginal additional cost (eg Telecom Gold charge a £10 telex registration fee and 5.5p per 100 characters for outgoing telexes). The facility also allows you to transmit telexes directly to 'dedicated' telex users (see page 120). (By the way, don't confuse 'teletex' with 'teletext': the latter is the name for the BBC and IBA non-interactive text data broadcast channels.)

Viewdata

This consists of 'pages' of information of all kinds. Prestel (soon to be renamed Vasscom X25) is the largest public database in the country. There are also private database services which can be subscribed to but are not normally accessed by the general public, the services provided by airlines to travel agents being one example.

The system is interactive to a limited extent. You can transmit message responses back to the information base using the computer keyboard. Thus you can carry out 'home banking' and 'home shopping' without ever leaving the house. At present there is little scope for using the facility in expanding a home-secretarial service, but it has interesting possibilities for the future.

The cost varies according to the service. Prestel users pay the cost of the telephone call and a supplement for the time connected to the service. Private viewdata services are either free (apart from telephone time) or are subject to a subscription fee.

Facsimile

This can best be described as a long-range photocopier. The system scans the original (which may be a typed document, a drawing or diagram) and sends signals via the public telephone network to a remote destination where the 'copy' is reproduced on a suitable fax machine. This may be useful if you have customers

121

who want to send copies of drawings or diagrams long distances very quickly. You should be able to obtain a basic fax machine for under £1000. You will also need special 'thermal' paper on which to receive facsimiles: this costs about £13 per roll.

An additional point in favour of offering a facsimile transmission service is that the recipient doesn't need his own facsimile machine in order to get copies quickly. The Post Office have a special service called Intelpost which allows you to transmit to the Intelpost office nearest the destination address from whence it can be collected or delivered within hours. Facsimile is another service which can now be linked to a computer network.

Selling the services to customers

The potential range of possible openings is endless. You can offer telex, electronic mail, telemessage and facsimile services to businesses and individuals who would otherwise not have access to these services. Many thousands of companies and private individuals currently subscribe to electronic mail/telex networks and this is likely to be an important communications link in the future.

For travelling businesspeople a small, portable computer/modem would allow them to link into the system wherever they were (provided there was a telephone) and they could either leave messages for you or interrogate their mailbox for messages from you. Remote customers who were also subscribers but lacked secretarial skills or a printer could forward rough drafts (in text form) for you to print, format, correct, print and post. (You could advertise such a service to the other subscribers by leaving a message in their mailboxes!)

You will need to undertake a careful costing and marketing exercise before starting up a service like this. Make sure that there is (or that you can generate) sufficient demand for these facilities in your area to more than cover the cost of providing them. You will also need to decide *how* you will charge for these communications services. For regular users a retaining fee plus a small charge each time the service is used would be appropriate, with a higher, one-off, charge for the one-only customer.

Audio-typing

This is another very lucrative sideline service you can offer for very little cost. Don't be put off if you have no experience; it is really very easy to learn and you will be able to teach yourself how to audio-type once you have the equipment. You will need a very good command of English grammar, spelling and punctuation if you are to undertake audio-typing and will have to make a conscious effort to avoid bad habits such as looking at the keyboard or typing point (you don't have copy to concentrate on and will need to fix your attention elsewhere).

Unlike copy typing, where you may actively *avoid* taking an interest in the meaning of the text, while audio-typing you will need to understand the sense of the sentence in order to avoid silly mistakes with similar sounding words such as bear/bare, forth/fourth, bored/board, formally/formerly, and so on. Ask your customers to speak clearly and distinctly, to indicate punctuation and paragraphing throughout the dictation and to provide a list (in dictation order) of spellings of real names, place names and specialist terms.

Chapter 7 deals with the equipment you will need and the variety of customers who will use such a service. Charge extra for the service itself and for providing the use of any dictation machinery and tapes.

Other services

If you are good at something – use it. There is no end to the range of skills that can be usefully combined with typing to improve the scope of your service and the income you can derive from it.

Translating
Publishers, large organisations, universities etc frequently require translations of books, reports, technical data and so on. The ability to translate the material *and* provide a perfectly typewritten copy will be invaluable. Write direct to likely organisations offering your services and specifying the language(s) in which you deal. Rates of pay vary considerably. In general, Chinese and Japanese translators are the best paid, European language translators the worst.

Teaching
If you can do it the chances are you can teach someone else business skills. There are a great many people who are interested in learning how to type, not necessarily to use a typewriter but to improve their keyboard skills so as to make computer programming easier and quicker. You may also be able to offer courses in word-processing or computer programming. A good

way to find out what is involved is to take one of these courses yourself, especially if it is some years since *you* learned how to type. You will also need to provide a suitable learning manual and the use of a machine for your students, as well as devising an appropriate course structure and timetable. Try advertising in the local press, shop windows and display boards. You should be able to earn £5–£10 per hour teaching a class of two to eight people.

English and specialist terminologies
Perhaps you are very good at spelling, grammar and punctuation. You could offer to rewrite reports, dissertations, letters and so on for an additional charge. Likewise, if you have a knowledge of any specialist terminologies (medical, legal etc) you might consider offering your services to doctors, solicitors, and other professional people.

Proof-reading
If you are very good at spotting typographical errors you might like to consider offering your services to publishers. Unfortunately this is a difficult market to get into as those publishers who use external proof-readers usually have a good supply already, and prefer people with good publishing experience. You could try writing to several publishers offering your services (you will find a list in the *Writers' and Artists' Yearbook*, published by A and C Black).

You might stand a better chance of getting your name known among publishers if you can do proof-reading for local writers; ask them to recommend you to their publishers. Take advantage of any specialist knowledge or training you may have. If you are conversant with medical terminology, for example, you may stand a better chance of entering the market if you write to publishers who specialise in medical textbooks emphasising your ability to proof-read medical manuscripts accurately. Publishers adopt certain house rules with regard to abbreviation, spelling, numbering, use of capital letters and so on. A copy of *Hart's Rules for Compositors* (Oxford University Press) will also be useful.

Indexing
Most non-fiction books have indexes and someone has to prepare them. Again, this is a difficult market to get into and persistence is necessary. You can improve your chances by taking a correspondence course with the Rapid Results College which will lead to a qualification in indexing and membership of the Society

of Indexers (who will also help you to get work). It is a specialised subject and certainly not an easy option. The work is often erratic but the pay, for a qualified indexer, is upwards of £5 per hour. Once a manuscript is in page proof, the index is required as soon as possible, so you will often have periods when there is no indexing to do interspersed with periods when you have to work 14 hours a day to meet the deadline for an index for a large work. Once again, if you have a specialist knowledge in a particular area, you may stand a better chance. Apply to publishers who deal with your specialist subject.

Typesetting

The revolution in computer technology has produced a situation whereby a home-typist with a computer/word processor and suitable typesetting software can typeset material, save it on a disc and forward this direct to a printer. You need to be a *very* good typist and proof-reader to undertake this type of work as the stored text will normally be converted directly into the proofs of a book, magazine, leaflet or whatever, and be printed photographically as the finished product. You may need to join one of the printing unions as many printers will not accept work from non-union typesetters. The work is usually well paid (but rates vary considerably according to the type of job). Work can be obtained from publishers, design consultants, advertising agents and so on.

Chapter 10

Expanding Your Business

Once your typing service is established and you have a good, regular supply of work you may want to consider expanding your service rather than turning work away because you are fully booked. You can do this very simply and easily from home and it is an excellent stepping stone to opening your own secretarial agency.

If you are advertising effectively and providing a good service you should almost always have an excess of work – that is, you should regularly have to turn work away because you are working to capacity. On the other hand, you may have geared your service to seasonal work-loads whereby you do most of your work during a certain period of the year with little or no work in the interim. Even so, you will probably find that during your seasonal peaks you are offered far more work than you can reasonably cope with alone.

There are a number of ways in which you can use overflow in order to increase your profit. The most obvious method is to work longer hours yourself. Another, less strenuous idea is to subcontract your work to others. This is not quite the same as offering other self-employed home-typists work that you cannot fit in yourself. An agreement with other home-typists (who advertise for themselves and run their own businesses) that you will pass on overflow work to each other does not usually involve one typist actually working 'for' the other. The advantage is that excess work will be distributed between them (where each will charge the customer directly) and not be lost entirely to another source.

Subcontracting

When you subcontract work to another party *you* remain responsible to the customer for the delivery and quality of the finished product and *you* invoice the customer for payment. The person who actually does the typing is paid by you but is not your employee – she is working in a self-employed capacity, just as you are. This sort of agreement can work very well. There are many skilled typists with time to spare who wish to make a little money working part time but do not want to become involved in setting up their own business. You may well have friends or acquaintances in this situation, or have come across such people in the course of running your own service.

Selecting subcontractors

The time when you suddenly find yourself with an excess of work that you cannot or do not want to turn away is *not* the time to start looking for a suitable subcontractor. The quality of the work your subcontractor turns out will reflect on *your* service and reputation, not theirs. You will want to spend some time making sure that whoever you choose for subcontracting work is suitably skilful, reliable and can produce work to the required standard.

Many home-typists ask friends or relatives to undertake excess typing work for them. This can be something of a mixed blessing. Whereas you may know the person concerned very well and be fully aware of her typing skills, you may also have great difficulty in providing the necessary guidance and criticism in the event of delays, errors or other problems associated with the work produced. One typist, during a seasonal flush of dissertations, asked his sister (who worked as a secretary for a firm of solicitors) to type some of the dissertations in her spare time. He offered a reasonable rate for the work (allowing a small profit for himself) and loaned her a typewriter. Many of the dissertations were urgent and the typist had guaranteed that they would be done on time. Unfortunately, his sister found the work much more demanding than she had anticipated and backed out of her agreement after the first dissertation. To make matters worse the typist found that the dissertation that *had* been typed was very badly done and he had to retype it. He didn't have the heart to complain and paid the agreed rate for the first dissertation anyway. Although this typist *did* manage to get all the dissertations completed on time by working extremely long hours for many weeks, the finished result was far below his usual high standards. The answer is not to offer work to your family or friends unless you are certain that they can do the work satisfactorily in the required time.

Advertising for subcontractors is sometimes effective. Secretarial students are often happy to take on spare-time work of this kind (try advertising on college or university notice boards). You could also put an advertisement in the 'Work Offered' section of your local newspaper. It might be wise to use a box number for replies otherwise you may find yourself swamped with telephone calls. If you do advertise for subcontractors you will have to ensure that they understand that you are *not* offering them employment. The money they earn from you will be treated as self-employed earnings and they will have to deal with their own income tax and National Insurance payments. It is also better, to avoid subcontractor *v* employee disagreements, if the subcontractors use their own equipment and work on their own premises. You will also want to be satisfied with their typing skills, discretion and reliability.

Sort through your replies and select half-a-dozen likely applicants. Although you will not need to conduct the formal sort of interview that would be necessary for employees, you will want to see candidates personally to discuss both your requirements and their availability. You should also ask them to complete a simple typing test and perhaps a proof-reading test to satisfy yourself that they are reasonably competent. Once you have decided on one or two potential subcontractors you should write to the other applicants thanking them for their interest and either declining their offers or informing them that you will bear them in mind for future work.

Using subcontractors

Try to avoid giving a new subcontractor a very long, complicated or important piece of work. Reserve these for yourself. Offer subcontractors (especially those doing their *first* piece of work for you) assignments in which the odd mistake will not matter too much and which you yourself can check quickly before passing on to the customer. Initial drafts, envelope addressing and straightforward repeat letters are most suitable.

Make sure your subcontractors are fully aware of your standards and requirements. If necessary, provide samples of the way you want the work laid out and ensure that your subcontractors know *when* you expect them to complete the assignment. You should also stress the need for confidentiality. Your subcontractors should, ideally, feel the same need to provide a first class, confidential service that you do. Don't be afraid to delegate to an established and obviously competent subcontactor. Just like employees, good subcontractors will do their best when they have an interest and incentive in the work and when they feel their abilities are valued.

Paying subcontractors

The rate you agree to pay your subcontractor(s) will obviously be less than you charge your customer. Apart from allowing for your costs: providing paper, wear and tear on your typewriter (if you provide one), electricity (if the subcontractor works on your premises), collection and delivery of work and advertising, you should make an allowance for the time you spend dealing with the customer (and any time spent explaining the work to the subcontractor) and for your own proof-reading of the finished work (this should only be necessary the first few times you use a subcontractor). After deducting these costs from the estimated charge to the customer you should also make an allowance for your own profit (say 10 per cent) before deciding how much you can pay the subcontractor for the work.

Obviously, your subcontractors will want to know how much you are going to pay them *before* they undertake the work so you will have to make a careful estimate of your own costs, fees and profit margins beforehand. It is probably better to err on the side of underpaying your subcontractors initially. It is much more satisfactory if you find you can increase their rate of payment later on, rather than have to ask them to accept a reduced rate for subsequent work because you have not estimated your costs (of which paying them is included) accurately enough.

Don't feel mean because your subcontractor is earning less for doing the work than you would be if you were doing it personally. Your subcontractors, remember, are not taking the risks – they are not paying for advertising, paper or the maintenance of equipment. They do not have to deal with customers or keep detailed business records. In addition, they may have a lower requirement for a high, regular, income. For many subcontractors, typing is likely to be very much a part-time pin-money affair. They can take it or leave it, and do not have to suffer the same responsibility if the work is badly done, or not done at all, that *you* are accepting when you take the work on. So don't feel guilty. On the other hand, you won't keep good, reliable, subcontractors if you pay them a very poor rate while you yourself are making a substantial profit on your charges to the customer (especially if they find out how much *you* were paid by the customer – and this is not as difficult as you might think).

Some subcontractors can be rather unscrupulous and may eliminate you as the 'middle-man' by going directly to your customer and offering to undertake the work for a reduced rate (more than you were paying, but less than you were charging the customer). This is, fortunately, a very rare occurrence (partly because the subcontractor can usually only get away with it once) but can be rather distressing. One way to avoid it is either to ensure that your subcontractor does not have access to your customer's name and address (which can be difficult, if not impossible) or to make sure that the subcontractor is not given very expensive assignments, or a lot of work for *one* customer where eliminating you could prove to be very lucrative.

Going into partnership

Taking on one or more partners is an obvious alternative to subcontracting but needs very careful consideration. The advantages, relative to subcontracting, are that your partner will have an equal stake in the typing service and will therefore have a greater incentive to work hard, keep deadlines and meet commitments than a subcontractor would. On the other hand, *your* profit may not increase very much, if at all, if you take on a partner rather than a subcontractor. After all, your partner will probably expect to take the same profit as you do. Thus your business may expand in terms of work and cash flow, but your own personal earnings may not increase at all.

Choosing a partner

Some of the factors you should consider when choosing a partner were outlined in Chapter 2. In general, partnerships in which the partners have complementary rather than similar skills seem to work best. If you are a whizz at typing accurately and fast but find it difficult to deal with customers or handle the organisation of your business, an outgoing and efficient partner who found it easy to deal with customers and administration would be ideal for you. If you're a poor proof-reader, pick a partner who is a good one. If you've bought a computer and can use it very well as a word processor but haven't a clue about extending its use in other ways, pick a partner who knows about computers (but perhaps can't type) in order to offer a range of computer services as well as word-processing.

As well as skills and abilities, you should consider the personality and character of your potential partner. You may have known someone personally for years but getting on well socially is no guarantee that you will be able to work together effectively as partners. *Before* you form a partnership, sit down with the person(s) concerned and discuss exactly who is going to do what in the business, how profits will be split, how costs will be met, and so on. It is relatively easy to decide on the general things; problems tend to arise over specific things, such as who is going to type up an assignment that *neither* partner likes, whose name will come first in advertisements, how the work-load will be split, who will be responsible for making purchases or writing up the books. Will the partners take customers in turn as they come in or will each partner deal exclusively with a particular group of customers and how will profits be allocated under such a system? What will happen if one partner feels that she or he is doing more work, or works faster than the other? What about the tips and gratuities that satisfied customers frequently bestow on valued typists? How will these be divided, if at all? Matters such as these, if left undecided, can cause a great deal of friction.

Legal aspects
Apart from the practical aspects of actually getting along with your partner, you should also consider your legal position. However small your typing service, you would be wise to have a formal partnership agreement drawn up by a solicitor. This defines the relationship between the partners and with third parties and will protect the partners in the event of any dispute or breakdown in the relationship. The Department of Employment in their leaflet 'Starting Your Own Business — the practical steps' (issued free by the Small Firms Service) recommend that a partnership agreement should include the following minimum details.

- Name and nature of business and commencing date.
- The amount of capital to be provided by each partner.
- The role of each partner clearly defined.
- The apportioning (equal or unequal shares) of profits and losses.
- Voting rights: how will decisions be made? Will one partner have overall control or will each have equal voting rights?
- The duration of the partnership.
- Arrangements for dissolving the partnership or releasing a partner.
- Provision for admitting new partners or getting rid of an existing partner.
- Arrangements for arbitration if the partners disagree.
- Arrangements concerning the retirement or death of a partner.

- How the bank account is to be operated.
- The preparation and auditing of annual accounts.
- What provision is to be made in the event of prolonged absence of a partner through sickness or accident.
- Insurance against death or sickness of a partner and for the business generally.

Another important point, noted in Chapter 2 but well worth repeating here, is that partners are held responsible for each other's debts (in relation to the typing service) and this also applies to income tax liability. If your partner fails to pay his or her share of income tax, the Inland Revenue can ask *you* to pay it.

If your partnership uses a business name you will need to comply with the requirements of the Companies Act 1981 in the same way as sole traders (see Chapter 2).

Chapter 11

Starting a Secretarial Agency

Coping with a large business tends to demand rather different skills from coping with a small one. The risks are also correspondingly greater.

Running your secretarial service from home requires the minimum of capital investment, enormous flexibility in terms of working hours and the type of work taken on, and can be run entirely single-handed on a very low budget. Once you decide to open a secretarial bureau you will need to reassess not only your own skills and abilities, but also the financial commitment required, the potential market (which will be different from that of a home-based secretarial agency) and prepare an entirely new financial forecast for the business.

Bringing in the professionals

Your home-based service was probably such a low risk affair that you didn't feel it necessary to consult the usual expert sources before embarking on it. Although a town centre service, properly researched, should have as much chance of success as a home-based service, the financial and legal implications require you to take a much longer and more serious look at your chances of success *before* you embark on the project. Had your home-based typing service been a disaster you would have lost very little (perhaps the cost of a typewriter and a few reams of paper – which you would probably be able to sell quite easily anyway); if your office-based service fails you may suffer much greater financial loss, especially if you have a large loan or overdraft and have purchased a lot of expensive (perhaps difficult to sell) equipment.

The bank manager
This is probably the first person you will wish to consult. Your own personal bank, or the one you have been using for your business account so far, is probably the best one to use. As well as the usual financial advice, and the ability to arrange loans or

overdrafts as necessary, your bank manager may be able to offer you advice on many commercial and business matters. He or she may have a good knowledge of local affairs and other business establishments.

If you require a loan or overdraft to purchase equipment for the agency, your bank manager will want to see a detailed financial forecast (along the lines described in Chapter 2) for the new business. Take along the accounts for your current home-based service as well. These will demonstrate not only your entrepreneurial ability, but also the accuracy of your previous financial forecasting together with the success you have already achieved in a business of this kind. All the banks have kits which show you how to produce a suitable business plan and it may be a good idea to ask for one of these in advance so that you are fully prepared before you approach the manager. Consultations with and advice provided by your bank manager are normally free.

Accountant

You may already be using an accountant to prepare your annual accounts (although this is not a statutory requirement for sole traders or partnerships). If so, you may want to consider asking his advice on a number of other matters related to the financial side of your proposed secretarial agency such as buying or leasing premises, keeping your tax liability to a minimum, employing staff, and so on.

If you don't already have an accountant to prepare your accounts and tax returns you may consider engaging one once you start a secretarial agency. Although the principles will be the same, the accounts will probably be rather more complicated because additional factors such as staff, premises, creditors and debtors will have to be taken into account. Your accountant will also help to prepare a financial forecast for presentation to your bank and can provide management accounts which will help you to see how the agency is going and how it could be improved.

Whether you take an accountant's advice or not, remember it's *your* business – *you* must decide how it is run. Your accountant can advise you but he can't guarantee your success. Take advice by all means, but make the decisions yourself. Consultations with accountants can be expensive. A freelance accountant will normally charge less than a large firm. Ask about fees before the consultation and don't forget to get an invoice and receipt so that you can charge it to your business.

Solicitor

The volume of legislation concerning industry and commerce is far too wide in scope and complex in detail for the busy owner of a secretarial agency to have time to understand it all. Solicitors tend to specialise so you would be well advised to use one knowledgeable in commercial and employment law. Most family solicitors are *not* normally involved in these aspects; however, your personal solicitor may be able to put you in touch with another who does specialise in this field. A firm of commercial solicitors with partners who are specialists in different branches of the law is your best bet.

As with accountants, the services of a good commercial law solicitor can be expensive, but lack of specialist advice could lead to heavy losses.

Insurance broker

As noted in Chapter 2, insurance is such a complicated business that you would be well advised to consult an insurance broker who will be able to tell you which insurances are necessary and which are desirable for your particular agency.

The services of an insurance broker are free and his advice should be impartial. Brokers also carry professional indemnity insurance which means you can sue them if their advice is so bad that you lose money as a consequence.

Get two or three quotes. Before you accept any proposals ask your accountant for advice on the tax aspects of the insurance. If you have been running a typing service from your home for some time you will probably already have insurance cover for your equipment and to cover customers and any employees. This will need to be revised when you start a secretarial agency. There are many types of insurance for businesses. Employer's liability insurance is required by law. Others of possible interest include public liability, fidelity guarantee (covering fraud by employees), fire, theft, personal accident, sickness, legal costs, health and pensions etc. 'Packaged' insurances are available for small businesses in which one policy covers your premises, equipment, personal insurance, employer's and public liability and so on at less cost than individual policies. Ask your broker about these.

Free professional help and advice

If you didn't feel the need to take advice when you started your home-typing service you will certainly want to do so now. Details of free help and advice available to new and existing small businesses can be found in Chapter 2.

Buying an existing agency

You may want to consider buying or leasing an existing secretarial bureau. There are advantages in this. First, you will save time and effort in setting up your own establishment with equipment and supplies. You may also acquire customers accustomed to trading with the previous owner. You will eliminate the waiting period during which you are too busy to continue your home-based business but haven't yet set up or attracted sufficient custom to your office-based service. The owner may also be prepared to offer you advice based on his or her experience in the business and buying an existing service may work out cheaper than renting or buying an office which has to be converted, decorated and equipped from scratch.

The benefits may be offset by disadvantages, however. The owner may have had a bad reputation with customers and/or creditors which you will have to overcome before you can make the service successful. The location may be poor or the service lacking sufficient custom. Ask yourself why the owner wants to sell the business – does the reason sound genuine? Does he or she intend to set up another typing (or related) service in the town? The fixtures, fittings and equipment may be outdated or in bad condition. You may not want to adopt someone else's business – especially if your own home-based service has been a great success and you have established customers of your own – although it is possible to change the name of the business, and announce the new ownership.

Examine the equipment carefully, determine its age and obtain evaluations of similar machines. Find out if parts and service agreements are still available. Check whether the equipment has been fully paid for and whether the business has any outstanding debts. Will the owner leave the present telephone number and the name of the business or will these need to be changed? Are the premises owned or leased? How long does the lease run and who actually owns the premises? Ask to see copies of all the relevant documents – lease, receipts for equipment, service/maintenance contracts, guarantees and so on, as well as the business's annual accounts. Check whether the local authority has any future development plans for the area; these may have a dramatic effect (positive or negative) on your service.

If you do decide to buy an existing agency have the sales agreement drawn up by a solicitor. It should include a description of what is being sold, the purchase price, the method of payment, the buyer's assumption of transferable maintenance agreements and guarantees, and a covenant with the seller not to compete within a certain period of time. If the service is still in operation then the agreement should also include the date and procedures of closing/re-opening under the new ownership.

If you buy an existing secretarial business, you will probably be asked to pay something for the 'goodwill'. This represents the value of business which may come to you as a result of the previous owner's efforts. Discuss this with your professional adviser and check whether existing customers are likely to keep on coming to you before the sum is agreed.

Above all, if you are thinking about buying an existing typing service take the advice of your solicitor or accountant. The legal process of handing over the business in exchange for cash or a loan should in any case be handled by a solicitor. Taking professional advice may involve a small expense but *not* taking it can be very costly indeed.

Starting afresh

If you don't want to buy an existing business (or there isn't one for sale in your area) you should consider buying or renting suitable premises. Buying premises is probably not a very good idea at the start as it ties up your capital; selling could be difficult and time-consuming should you need to dispose of the property quickly. On the other hand, commercial leases, unlike domestic ones, run for relatively short periods: usually between three and seven years with rent reviews at the end of each term or sooner. This adds an unknown factor to the long-term future of a secretarial bureau in rented premises. You will need to look at the advantages and disadvantages of both before deciding on the best option for you.

Finding premises
There are several options open to you when you are looking for potential premises. Newspapers are a good place to start. Commercial and business properties are advertised in publications such as *Dalton's Weekly*. Local evening newspapers usually contain advertisements for local business and commercial premises. Sometimes local councils have premises – which can be made available – occasionally with rent-free periods. Another good source of information about locally available premises is an enterprise agency.

Location and suitability of premises

You will probably want to locate in the business or commercial centre of your town. When considering premises, several points should be borne in mind, including whether your service will be visible from the street (this can have important consequences for the number of customers you can attract), how easily your customers will be able to reach it as well as the number and size of the rooms available, the state of decoration and repair, the toilet/washroom/kitchen facilities and requirements to comply with fire safety regulations (which may affect any internal alterations you have in mind). You will also want to find out what, if any, competition you will have in the immediate area.

As well as the length and cost of any lease, you will need to consider the amount required for internal decoration and fittings and external sign painting. Check whether the lessor is prepared to make a contribution towards any redecoration, repair or alteration required. Think about the amount of space you are going to need. How many desks will you have? How much space do you need to provide for photocopiers, display stands, printers and seating for customers? How will the space available be divided up? You may need planning permission if starting your secretarial bureau will entail a change of use of the premises you have selected. Be sure to check what the existing planning use is. If in doubt, consult either your solicitor or the planning office of your local authority.

Once you have one or two suitable premises in mind it can be a good idea to make a diagram (on squared paper) of the internal layout. Cut out proportionally sized shapes corresponding to the fittings and equipment you have in mind and see how these would fit. You will also want to consider the number and positions of sockets and lighting points (a secretarial service will need a lot of these).

Will you have a separate room in which customers can discuss their needs in confidence if necessary, or will you conduct all your business in a large open office? Do you want premises with a small office frontage and reception desk where customers can be dealt with, while keeping the main bulk of the equipment and work space out of sight? Look at other secretarial/typing services – how are the offices laid out? Which ones appear to offer the most attractive and professional service?

Furnishing and decor

Once you have selected your premises you will need to think about furnishing and decor. While it would be wasteful to spend vast sums creating your ideal office environment it would be equally rash to start your secretarial agency in tatty, poorly furnished surroundings. The image you create, especially in the reception area, will influence both potential and existing customers. Your offices should be clean, airy and uncluttered. It may be worth investing in new carpeting and perhaps having walls and ceilings emulsioned. (Perhaps you could offer to do some typing or printing in return for decorating services?)

Again, it is not strictly necessary to buy new desks for yourself and your staff. Good quality second-hand desks should look good and will last longer than brand new but inferior ones. Spend more on the reception area and display stands and on ensuring that any window display area is well decorated and attractive; you might like to consider including plants and comfortable chairs, especially if customers have to wait for service or photocopies. You can now buy large tubs of imitation plants which look very realistic but need no maintenance (apart from the odd wash). They are about as expensive as the real thing, but tend to survive an office environment rather better!

Keep looking good

There is little point in decorating your offices and providing attractive lighting, seating and displays if you then let it become run-down, dirty or untidy. Make sure that any areas where customers have access, or can see, are kept clean and free from disorganised piles of paper. Make arrangements to have any windows cleaned once a fortnight or so and either clean the interior of the offices yourself or hire a cleaner to do the job for you daily. Make sure your staff understand that papers, rubbish, cups of tea and take-away meals are not to be taken to, or left in, the reception area.

Stock and equipment

Your equipment needs will be dictated by the size and range of services you are initially going to offer. You will certainly need a minimum of two typewriters (or equivalent), two desks, a filing cabinet, a reception desk (higher than a conventional desk because it is intended to be *stood* at), a photocopier (virtually all typing/secretarial services would be expected to be able to provide photocopies), typists' and customers' chairs and storage cupboards.

Starting afresh in a new secretarial business is a good opportunity to take advantage of the new technology that is currently revolutionising office equipment. Chapter 7 gives details of some of this new office technology. Magazines such as *Which Computer?*, *Which Wordprocessor?*, *Practical Computing* and *Computer Age* provide up-to-date details of new computerised technology while the annual Daily Mail *Office Automation Guide* gives more comprehensive coverage of the variety of modern office equipment. The Small Firms Service issues a free guide entitled 'Microprocessors and the Small Business'. You may want to consider offering electronic printing services using one of the new computerised laser-printer/photocopier desk top systems that are currently retailing for about £3000. These can be used for graphics, typesetting, magazine quality printing, collating and so forth. Add a binding machine and you will have a high quality printing service in addition to typing and photocopying.

You may also need to reconsider your stock suppliers. While you were working from home, and especially while you were working alone, your stock turnover will have been relatively slow and you may have been quite content to buy everything from local suppliers. Your town centre secretarial agency should have a much higher turnover than your home-based business and you will therefore need to investigate bulk suppliers. You may find that you can have bulk supplies, delivered to your premises, much more cheaply by large wholesalers than the small stationers you have been dealing with. Once again, time spent researching suppliers and costs will be invaluable later on. While you are enquiring, ask about discounts, credit facilities and advertising displays.

Costing, pricing and estimating

You will need to reassess completely your costs following the same basic rules you used (Chapter 4) for your home-based service. Your basic costs will be very much higher once you start operating a secretarial agency. Rent, rates, wages, maintenance of premises, higher insurance premiums, fees for professional services, loan repayments and so on, will all increase your cost-per-job rate. This means that you will have to start charging your customers a higher rate – especially if you also need (or want) to start charging VAT.

As a town centre agency you will have many more customers than a home-based typing service and the fact that you will probably be offering a wider range of extra facilities means that your new venture should be as successful, hopefully more so, than your old one. Ironically, you will probably find that most customers are prepared to pay more, wait longer for completion and be rather less 'finicky' about minor errors and corrections than they would be when dealing with a home-based typist! Don't let this make you complacent. You are in the big league now and will need to keep on your toes if you are not going to let your competitors attract the majority of the market.

Chapter 12

Taking on Staff

Once your typing business has progressed beyond the one-person operation stage, and certainly once you have established yourself in separate business premises, you will have to deal with the selection, motivation and training of staff. As well as your legal responsibilities you will have to tackle all aspects of working relations including discipline, dismissal, health and safety of staff, negotiating wages, hours of work and leave.

Before you advertise for staff you will need to consider carefully what kind of skills your employees will need, how many hours you need them to work and what (and how) you can pay them. Write a job description for each employee. This will help you to clarify what skills your employees will need, will be useful during interviews when you can specify exactly what will be required, and will help you to formulate your advertisements.

Selecting staff

In a small business where commitment is so important, good working relations crucial and the margin for error small, finding the right staff is vital. There are several ways to find suitable candidates. You may already know someone who would be suitable: perhaps someone who has subcontracted for you in the past would be interested. Alternatively, you can advertise in local shop windows or local newspapers. Private employment agencies are another possibility, although they may charge you a fee (often a percentage of your employee's starting salary) for finding a suitable applicant. Your local Jobcentre/employment exchange will advertise your vacancies and will tell you if suitable people are registered with them, but tend not to be very selective when they refer staff to you.

It will help if you can give the Jobcentre full details of the work involved, wages, qualifications needed, training offered, and so on. Similarly, the more information you can put in your advertisements the better potential applicants will be able to assess their suitability for the job, and the job's suitability for them.

In the present economic climate you will probably receive a large number of applications – even for a part-time job that is not exceptionally well paid – so you will need to have a method of sifting through these to select the most appropriate candidates for interview. Don't automatically plump for the highest qualified applicants or those who are prepared to work for the lowest wages: they may simply use you as a stepping stone to more lucrative employment. You want employees who are dedicated, adaptable and versatile. You are most likely to get these if you provide the right incentives (not just money) and if you show your willingness to help them develop their potential in the job.

An application form (which you can devise and photocopy or print yourself) has the advantage of standardising the information collected from applicants and ensuring that each applicant covers all the questions you want answered. On the other hand, if you ask applicants to apply in writing you may get a better idea of their ability in English, writing, composition and so.

In any event you should make notes of any questions you want answered during interview (from gaps in the application form or written application). If possible, after selecting two or three possibles from the first interview, hold a second interview. Finding the right staff is critical for a small secretarial service so it is as well to take plenty of time over the selection. You may want to include a typing/shorthand/audio test during the first interview and will be looking, among other things, for punctuality, a neat appearance, confidence and an outgoing, helpful personality. If the applicant is likely to be left in charge of the bureau at any time, you need to be sure he or she has the maturity and ability to handle any eventuality. Does the applicant have appropriate abilities and qualifications? Can he/she deal with customers personally and on the telephone? Does he/she understand the degree of commitment and flexibility that is required in working for a small business?

Once you have made your selection you will want to offer the job immediately. Do this by telephone and confirm in writing (and ask the prospective employee to accept the offer in writing within a certain time). Be sure to take up references *before* you offer the job, or make the receipt of satisfactory references a condition of the appointment. In the offer, restate the basic terms of the employment (date of commencement, hours, salary, leave etc). You will also need to reject unsuccessful candidates. Write a simple, polite, rejection letter after you have a firm acceptance: don't go into the details of *why* they were unsuccessful.

Discrimination on the grounds of race of sex

If you employ fewer than six people you are normally exempt from the sex discrimination provisions when taking on staff but you must not discriminate on the grounds of race. It is a good idea to take full notes of your decisions and reasons during interviews so that you can show, if necessary, your reasons for selecting one candidate in preference to another.

Contracts of employment

As soon as someone starts working for you, you have a legal contract with that person, whether or not anything is written down. (Your advertisement, job description and anything you say during interview can be held to be part of that contract, so don't make rash statements.) Within 13 weeks of commencement you must provide the employee(s) with a written statement of the main terms and conditions of their employment. This will include your name, the date continuous employment began, pay, hours of work, details of holidays, sick pay and pensions, period of notice, job title, disciplinary rules and grievance procedure. You do not have to provide a written statement to employees who normally work less than 16 hours per week (unless they have worked for you for more than eight hours per week for over five years).

Pay, tax and National Insurance

When deciding how much to pay your employees you will need to take into account not only how much you can afford, and think the work is worth to you, but also the going rate for similar jobs in your area.

You must inform the tax office which already deals with your business when you take on staff or they leave. They will tell you where your Pay As You Earn (PAYE) tax office will be and that office will send you the instructions and forms you need to operate PAYE and National Insurance. You will have to deduct tax from your employees' pay (under the PAYE system) and will be responsible for paying both the employer's and employee's Class 1 National Insurance contributions (you deduct the employees' contribution from their pay). Leaflet P7 'Employers Guide to PAYE', available from the Inland Revenue, and leaflet NP15 'Employers Guide to National Insurance Contributions' from the DHSS lay down the guidelines for these deductions.

You must provide each employee with a pay slip showing gross pay, itemising deductions, and giving the net sum to be received, on each pay day.

Hours of work, holidays and leave of absence

When deciding which hours, and how many per week your employee(s) will be needed you should consider when your peak daily work-loads occur, what provision you need to make for lunch breaks, whether you will be open on Saturday, and if you will have an early closing day. If you plan to start off with just yourself and one helper you should consider taking on two part-timers rather than one full-time employee. This gives you greater flexibility and means you won't be left completely single-handed in the event of holidays or sick leave.

Provisions for time off for attending ante-natal clinics, public duties, trade union activities, maternity and sick leave are covered in the leaflet 'Employing People' obtainable from the Small Firms Service.

You may need to make some provision for taking on temporary staff during employees' holidays and sick leave. 'Temps' are available from temporary staffing agencies but the fees are usually very high. A good alternative is to take on students (out of term time) or to advertise for suitably qualified temporary staff either in your local paper or through the Jobcentre. You may already hold a list of stand-by helpers.

Good working relations

You will get the best results from your employee(s) if you treat them as valuable members of your team rather than simple automatons expected to do little more than follow orders efficiently.

Get into the habit of delegating work: don't try to do everything yourself. Set high standards and provide adequate training and opportunities for your staff to reach them. Ask for your employees' counsel and help; give them a chance to take part in decisions and try to let them carry out their own ideas. If criticism is necessary, do it constructively. Suggest ways in which their work (or behaviour) could be improved rather than complaining about the faults.

Discipline and dismissal

If you discover a problem the first thing to do is to investigate it

145

fully; then tell your employee what the complaint is and give her/him a chance to explain her/his side of the problem. The formal procedure demands that you give the employee a verbal warning (confirm this in writing), followed by a final written warning before dismissal can take place, except for gross misconduct. You cannot fire someone if they are carrying out the requirements of the contract you have with them and beware of giving an inappropriate disciplinary warning.

One secretarial bureau had an employee who worked very well but was persistently late. The manageress eventually warned the employee that if she was not in on time for the next 30 days she would be sacked. The employee was punctual for 30 days and then, on the thirty-first day, was late again. She was sacked but went to a tribunal and won. It was a case of unfair dismissal because it was what was known as a 'resolutive warning'. What the manageress should have said was, 'You will be fired if you are late during the next 30 days and thereafter you will be expected to obey the standards demanded by the firm's rules.'

Employment legislation

Although the bulk of employment legislation is there to protect the employee, special provisions have been made in many cases (unfair dismissal, maternity leave, and so on) for small businesses. Often they are excluded from the necessity to comply with certain regulations.

In addition to the basic guide 'Employing People', the following pamphlets, available free from the Department of Employment, provide more detailed information about employment legislation:

No 1 Written statement of main terms and conditions of employment
No 2 Procedure for handling redundancies
No 3 Employee's rights in insolvency of employer
No 4 Employment rights for the expectant mother
No 8 Itemised pay statement
No 10 Employment rights on the transfer of an undertaking
No 11 Rules governing continuous employment and a week's pay
No 14 Rights to notice and reasons for dismissal

Copies of these and other publications are available from Jobcentres, Employment Offices and the Advisory, Conciliation and Arbitration Service (ACAS). ACAS also operate an advice service for employers; their address is in the telephone directory.

Health and safety

Office environments can seem relatively safe but there are hazards involved, especially in the operation of electrical equipment and machinery. Don't have electrical leads trailing over the floor or piles of paper standing around for months. Make sure potentially dangerous equipment (guillotines, paper shredders, electric staplers etc) have proper guards and that staff are instructed in safety procedures. Make sure that you have adequate insurance cover for staff, customers, premises and property in the event of accident.

The health and safety regulations are very extensive. Your local office of the Health and Safety Executive will tell you what your legal responsibilities are and a number of free guideline publications are available from them. Your local Fire Prevention Officers will advise you about the necessary fire precautions. Another useful source of advice and information is the Royal Society for the Prevention of Accidents, Cannon House, The Priory Queensway, Birmingham B4 6B6; 021-233 2461.

Chapter 13

Useful Addresses

Advisory, Conciliation and Arbitration Service (ACAS)
 11–12 St James's Square, London SW1Y 4LA; 01-214 6000
 Also regional offices: consult your local telephone directory.
Alliance of Small Firms and Self-Employed People
 42 Vine Road, East Molesey, Surrey KT8 9LF; 01-979 2293
Association of Medical Secretaries
 Tavistock House North, Tavistock Square, London WC1H
 9LN; 01-388 2648
BBC External Services
 PO Box 76, Bush House, Strand, London WC2B 4PH
 (translation/interpretation work)
British Insurance Brokers Association
 10 Bevis Marks, London EC3A 7LH; 01-623 9043
Business in the Community
 227A City Road, London EC1V 1JU; 01-235 3716
 and 25 St Andrew Square, Edinburgh EH1 2AF; 031-556
 9761
Companies Registration Office
 Companies House, Crown Way, Maindy, Cardiff CF4 3UZ;
 0222 388588
 and
 102 George Street, Edinburgh EH2 3DJ; 031-225 5774
 and
 Chichester House, 43–47 Chichester Court, Belfast BT1 4PJ;
 0232 234121
Council for Small Industries in Rural Areas (CoSIRA)
 141 Castle Street, Salisbury, Wiltshire SP1 3TP; 0722 336255
 Regional offices are listed in the telephone book
**The Institute of Scientific and Technical Communicators
Limited**
 17 Bluebridge Avenue, Brookmans Park, Hatfield,
 Hertfordshire AL9 7RY; 0707 55392

Law Society
  Legal Aid Department, 113 Chancery Lane, London WC2A
  1PL; 01-242 1222
Market Research Society
  15 Belgrave Square, London SW1X 8PF; 01-235 4709
**National Federation of Self-employed and Small Business
Ltd**
  32 St Anne's Road West, Lytham St Annes, Lancashire FY8
  1NY; 0253 720911
  and
  140 Lower Marsh, London SE1 7AE; 01-928 9272
Small Business Bureau
  32 Smith Square, London SW1P 3HH; 01-222 9000
Small Firms Service
Department of Employment
  Steel House, Tothill Street, London SW1H 9LN; 01-387
  6005
  The Department has a number of regionally based small firms
  centres: telephone 100 and ask for freefone Enterprise.
Northern Ireland
Local Enterprise Development Unit, Lamont House, Purdy's
  Lane, Newtownbreda, Belfast BT8 4TB; 0232 691031
The Scottish Development Agency
(Small Business Division), 102 Telford Road, Edinburgh EH4
  2NP; 031-343 1911
Highlands and Islands Development Board
Bridge House, 27 Bank Street, Inverness IV1 1QR; 0463
  234171
The Welsh Development Agency
(Small Business Division), Treforest Industrial Estate,
  Pontypridd, Mid Glamorgan CF37 5UT; 044 385 3131

Society of Indexers
Secretary: Mrs C Robertson, 7A Parker Street, Cambridge
  CB1 1JZ; 0223 311913
Translators' Association
Society of Authors, 84 Drayton Gardens, London SW10 9SD;
  01-373 6642

Chapter 14
Further Reading

Starting and running a business

Annual Audit and Annual Accounts, Adam Mills (Frederick Muller)
Be Your Own Boss: How to Become Self-employed, John Blundell
  (National Federation of the Self-employed)
Croner's Reference Book for the Self-Employed and Smaller Business,
  Croner Publications Limited, 173 Kingston Road, New
  Malden, Surrey KT3 3SS (on annual subscription)
Effective Advertising; The Daily Telegraph Guide for the Small Business,
  HC Carter (Kogan Page)
The Guardian Guide to Running a Small Business, 6th edition, Ed
  Clive Woodcock (Kogan Page)
A Handbook of New Office Technology, 2nd edition, John Derrick
  and Phillip Oppenheim (Kogan Page)
Law for the Small Business, 5th edn, Patricia Clayton (Kogan
  Page)
Partnership, I Stratton and I Blackshaw (Oyez)
Running Your Own Business, Richard Edwards (Oyez)
Starting a Successful Small Business, MJ Morris (Kogan Page)
Success in Bookkeeping for the Small Business, G Whitehead (John
  Murray)
A Woman's Guide to Starting Her Own Business, Susan Glasock
  (Granada)
The Word Processing Handbook, John Derrick and Phillip
  Oppenheim (Kogan Page)
Working for Yourself; The Daily Telegraph Guide to Self-employment,
  9th edition, Godfrey Golzen (Kogan Page)
The Working Office, Geoffrey Salmon (The Design Council)

Recommended reference works

A good dictionary, such as *The Concise Oxford Dictionary*, is
  essential.

A Dictionary of Modern English Usage, HW Fowler: useful for any
  problem relating to English grammar or usage.
Roget's Thesaurus of English Words and Phrases, Penguin. This
  lists words according to their meaning and is invaluable in
  helping you to choose the right one.
Whitaker's Almanack, an annual publication, containing factual
  information.

For those involved in medical work
Dorland's Pocket Medical Dictionary and/or *Baillière's Nurses'
  Dictionary*
The Medical Secretary's and Receptionist's Handbook, Michael Drury
  (Baillière Tindall)
Medical Shorthand Dictation Passages, Irene Burgess (Cassell) (for
  New Era shorthand practice).
Medical Words and Phrases, Janice Kerr (Pitman) (for Pitman
  2000 shorthand practice and reference).
MIMS Published monthly and sent to every GP, this contains a
  list of all proprietary drugs and will be invaluable when
  checking the spelling of some of these difficult names.

For those involved in legal work
The Legal Secretary's Handbook, A Newington and HM
  Willoughby (Oyez Longman)
A Secretary's Guide to Legal Office, Annette Parry (Pitman)
  (particularly for New Era and 2000 shorthand practice and
  reference).

For those involved in work for publication
Hart's Rules for Compositors and Readers (Oxford University Press)
The Oxford Dictionary for Writers and Editors (Oxford University
  Press)
Indexes and Indexing, R L Collison (Ernest Benn)

Books and magazines on secretarial skills

Learning to type
Applied Typing, Drummond and Scattergood (McGraw-Hill)
Compose and Type, Margaret Tombs (Pitman)
Typing First Course, Drummond and Scattergood (McGraw-Hill)
Universal Typing, Edith MacKay (Pitman)

Typewriting exercises are also included in the monthly *Memo 2000* and *Teeline* magazines

Audio-typing
Audio Transcription, Archie Drummond (McGraw-Hill)
Audio-typing. A Progressive Course, Edith Whicher (Pitman)
Elementary Audio-typing, Barbara Colley (Pitman)
Longman Audio Typing, Marion Prescott (Longman)

Shorthand theory and skill practice
Gregg Shorthand: *Gregg Speed Practice*, E W Crockett; *Today's Secretary Magazine* both published by McGraw-Hill.
New Era Shorthand: *Memo* magazine; *Office Skills* magazine; *The New Phonographic Phrase Book*, Emily D Smith, all published by Pitman.
Pitman 2000: *2000* magazine; *Office Skills* magazine; *Pitman 2000*; *Speedbuilder*.
Pitmanscript: *Progressive Shorthand Passages* (Books 1, 2, 3 and 4), M Quint; *Pitmanscript Graded Exercises*, Emily D Smith, both published by Pitman.
Teeline: *Teeline Shorthand Made Simple; First/Second Teeline Workbooks; Teeline Magazine*, all published by Heinemann.

Word processing
Introducing the Electronic Office, S G Price (National Computing Centre)
Making the Most of Word Processing, T H Chambers (Business Books)
Word Processing, M E Bradshaw and B M Garstang (Edward Arnold). Elementary and intermediate advanced workbooks for students.
Word Processing – A Systems Approach to the Office, McCabe and Popham (Harcourt Brace Jovanovich)
Word Processing in the Modern Office, Paula B Cecil (Benjamin/Cummings Publishing)

Magazines of general use and interest
Business Success (Parkway Publications); this contains some useful general articles (eg 'Selecting an Accountant'), advice column and new product coverage.
Business Systems and Equipment (Business Publications)
Memo and *Office Skills* (Pitman)

Practical Computing and *Computer Age*: useful for information on
new computer technology and software.
Which Word Processor? and *Which Computer?* (Business and
Computer Publishers)

Free leaflets and guides

There is an abundance of free literature available to established
and new small businesses, listed in *Sources of Free Business
Information* (Kogan Page). The following is a sample of the guides
most relevant to a typing service.

Small Firms Service
A Big Help to Small Businesses
Elements of Bookkeeping, L A Rich and T J Terry
Employing People
Marketing: a Guide for Small Firms, E G Wood
Microprocessors and the Small Business
Starting Your Own Business – The Practical Steps

Department of Health and Social Security
Leaflet NP15 *Employers Guide to NI Contributions*
Leaflet NI208 *National Insurance Contribution Rates*
Leaflet NI41 *National Insurance Guide for the Self-Employed*
Leaflet NP18 *Class 4 Contributions*
Leaflet NI27A *People with Small Earnings from Self-Employment*

Inspector of Taxes
IR28 *Starting in Business*
IR56 *Tax – Employed or Self-Employed*
P7 *Employers Guide to PAYE*
CGT11 *Capital Gains Tax and the Small Businessman*

Customs and Excise VAT Offices
700 *General Guide*
700/1/86 *Should I Be Registered for VAT?*
700/15/84 *The Ins and Outs of VAT*
700/21/86 *Keeping Records and Accounts*
701 *Scope and Coverage*
701/10/85 *Printed and Similar Matter*
706 *Self-supply (Stationery)*

Department of Employment
These titles are part of a series:

1. *Written statement of Main Terms and Conditions of Employment*
3. *Employees Rights on Insolvency of Employer*
4. *Employment Rights for the Expectant Mother*
8. *Itemised Pay Statement*
10. *Employment Rights on the Transfer of an Undertaking: the Law on Unfair Dismissal – Guidance for Small Firms*

Health and Safety Commission
Advice to Employers
Advice to the Self-Employed
The 1974 Act Outlined

Guide to Layout and Sample Formats

Dissertations, theses and manuscripts

Universities, polytechnics and colleges normally provide their degree students with a detailed specification for the format of dissertations and theses. This normally comprises instructions for page numbering, margins, footnotes, spacing, layout of bibliography, quotations, and so on. Publishers almost always provide similar instructions for their authors. Hence, if you are asked to type a dissertation, thesis, manuscript or play script, you should ask if your customer has received specific format instructions. Once you have typed one or two dissertations for a particular university you will know its requirements. It is a good idea to keep a note of these as many students mislay, or fail to receive, their dissertation typing instructions.

Dissertations and theses

As a general guide type on one side of A4 paper and leave a margin of about 35 mm on the left and about 25 mm on the other three sides. Dissertations and theses are normally bound (often with a simple grip binding) on the left and the extra margin width allows for this. Double-space the main text throughout and leave an extra line (or two) between paragraphs and between headings/sub-headings and text. Headings, sub-headings etc should be standardised throughout the text. Quotations, footnotes, references and bibliographies are normally single-spaced. Indent quotations about five spaces (at both sides) as well as any footnotes and references which appear in the main body of the text.

References to other works (eg book titles), species names and some medical terms are conventionally underlined (the student should already have done this on the handwritten copy). Numbering normally starts on the first page of the first chapter (this is usually preceded by a facing page showing the title, author, date, university and so on; an acknowledgements page and a contents page). You will have to type the contents page last as you will need to insert the relevant page numbers and you won't know these until the end. Start each new chapter on a new page. Normally two copies are required for submission and the student may wish to retain a third copy (photocopies are normally acceptable, as are properly corrected, clear carbons).

Book manuscripts

Book manuscripts are conventionally double-spaced throughout (including quotations, references and bibliography) on one side of A4 paper with four spaces between paragraphs, headings and text and sub-headings and text. This additional space makes it easier for the editor and typesetter to read, and mark comments on the script as well as allowing plenty of space for clear alterations or corrections. Likewise, leave generous margins all round and especially on the left where there should be extra space to allow for the typesetter's clip to hold the manuscript without obscuring the text. Publishers usually prefer manuscripts to be typed using a typeface with regular, rather than 'proportional' character spacing (ie each character taking up the same amount of space) as this makes it easier for the typesetter to estimate the amount of text on a page. All pages should be numbered, preferably consecutively. Occasionally the title page, preface, lists of contents, etc are numbered separately in roman numerals. Page numbers should be in the top right-hand corner. It is normally acceptable to insert extra pages later on so long as these are numbered appropriately (340a, 340b and so on in between pages 340 and 341 with a note on pages 340 *and* 341 that 340a and 340b follow and precede respectively). Two copies are normally required by the publisher (and the author would be well advised to keep a copy for him or herself). Good quality carbon copies are usually acceptable as are photocopies. Ask the author for a copy of the publisher's house rules regarding abbreviation, spelling, hyphenation, composite words, numbering, dates, addresses, titles and the use of capital letters. If the author has not followed the publisher's house rules you can offer to make the appropriate corrections (but be sure to charge extra): and remember to be consistent – it's not good enough to type 'book-keeping' on one page and 'bookkeeping' on the next.

Play scripts

You may be asked to type these for local amateur dramatic societies or, more rarely, for professional playwrights (who will have more stringent rules for the layout of the script). In general, you should leave a very generous margin on the left (40 mm or more): this allows sufficient room for binding and leaves the text clear for the performers to read. Separate dialogue from the rest of the script (scene changes, character descriptions, details of action, motivation, behaviour and so on) by leaving a space and indenting from the left as shown below:

TYPIST Leave a space between dialogue and

the rest of the script. Type

character names in capitals. Number

scene changes sequentially. Double-

space the dialogue for ease of

reading.

You should also consider the time it will take you to type a play script when you estimate your charges. It is much more difficult to type colloquial speech, for example, than it is to type literary, academic or business speech. The number of copies required will be determined by whether the play is for the direct use of an amateur dramatic society or is the preliminary script for a professional play, film or television programme.

Business letters

For business people who do not have fixed ideas about the layout of their correspondence you could provide a variety of sample displays.

Style

The principle popular letter styles are fully blocked and semi-blocked (see figures on page 158). A fully blocked letter is quicker and easier to type and also allows you to position the address so that a window envelope can be used (which provides a further saving in time since you don't have to type the address on an envelope).

Letters should be laid out and spaced according to their length.

Punctuation

Many businesses now use open punctuation. This means that no punctuation is inserted in the date, names, addresses, salutation

SUPERSONIC VAN HIRE LIMITED
Any Street, Anytown.

Semi-blocked letter

SUPERSONIC VAN HIRE LIMITED
Any Street, Anytown.

Fully-blocked letter

and complimentary close, or after contractions. This has the advantage of saving typing time but some people do not like it. Be guided by the preference of your customer.

Paragraphing
A new paragraph is used whenever the subject changes. many business people are hopeless at paragraphing and will appreciate your help with this. Avoid a letter in the form of a single long paragraph. Almost all letters can be broken down into at least three parts: the opening remarks, the bulk of the information being conveyed, and a summation requesting action.

The subscription
When the letter starts with 'Dear Sir/Madam' the subscription is 'Yours faithfully'; when the salutation is 'Dear Mr Jones' the subscription is 'Yours sincerely'.

Agendas and minutes

You may be asked to prepare agendas and minutes of meetings for local clubs and organisations. Usually the customer will provide an old agenda or set of minutes for your guidance: if so follow the layout of the previous ones. Be certain to ask how many copies will be required (normally each member of the committee has one and one should be retained by the chairman for filing). These are the standard headings that commonly appear on the agenda:

1. The place, date and time of the meeting
2. Apologies for absence
3. Minutes of last meeting (these will be read, confirmed as correct and signed by the chairman)
4. Business arising from the minutes
5. Main business of the meeting (possibly several sections on this)
6. Any other matters
7. Date of next meeting

The minutes of a meeting record the name of the board or committee, the place, date and time of the meeting. The members present are listed followed by those who send apologies for absence. (Take care to ensure that you can read the names of committee members: if necessary ask your customer to print these separately.) The minutes then follow the items on the agenda noting, in particular, any decisions that have been made.

Occasionally, an 'Action' column separated from the minutes by at least three spaces is used.

Curriculum vitae

The layout of CVs can vary but the essential ingredients generally remain the same. Most comprise the following general sections:

Personal details
Educational qualifications
Professional qualifications and memberships
Employment history
Interests and hobbies
Referees

You will want to tailor each CV to suit individual customers and their employment aspirations. However you lay out the CV you should aim to stress the applicant's strongest features and, if the applicant is applying for a particular type of job, emphasise qualities, qualifications and experience relevant to that particular career. Many people have difficulty in presenting information of this nature in the most attractive and readable form. So if you have good compositional English skills you should be able to make a great success of a CV production service.

Your charge will depend on whether you are simply typing up the customer's own handwritten résumé or whether you are actually composing the CV from the customer's details.

Make up a book of samples showing a variety of layouts (block out actual names/addresses to preserve confidentiality) and offer a selection of paper weights and colours. Include extra sheets for handwritten covering letters and matching envelopes for an 'executive' service.

Two examples are offered on pages 161 and 162. Try to avoid having your customer's CV extending beyond three or four pages. At this length your customer risks boring a potential employer with detail, unless the job is very specialised and a long breakdown of work experience is called for.

Basic curriculum vitae

<u>Name:</u>	JOHN DOE	<u>Date of Birth:</u>	15.05.1956
<u>Address:</u>	46 Any Street Anytown ANY 156	<u>Age:</u>	31
		<u>Status:</u>	Single
<u>Telephone:</u>	(0101) 34567	<u>Health:</u>	Excellent
		<u>Nationality:</u>	British

<u>Schools/College Attended</u>	<u>Qualification Received</u>
Anytown Grammar School Anytown 1967–1972	GCE 'O' levels in: Mathematics (A), English (B), Geography (B) and Physics (C)
Anytown College of FE Anytown 1972–1974	HNC Accounting

<u>Employer/Dates</u>	<u>Position/Responsibility</u>
AB Jones Hosiery Anytown 1980–present	OFFICE MANAGER Supervising staff of six. Total administrative control of advertising, sales, purchases, payroll and bookkeeping.
Anytown Council Council Anytown 1974–1980	CLERICAL ASSISTANT (1974–1976). Making up wage packets for 230 employees. Keeping employee records. CLERICAL OFFICER (1976–1980). Keeping inventory records, preparing and checking purchase orders, processing payments and receipts.

<u>Interests and Hobbies</u>

Squash, swimming, travel, reading and home-computing.

<u>Referees</u>

Available as required.

Expanded curriculum vitae

This would have the same personal and educational details as described in the 'basic' CV but would include an expanded section detailing work or other relevant experience as well as emphasising any particular apptitudes and abilities as shown below.

Employment History and Experience

1980–present   AB Jones Hosiery
                                                      Anytown

As OFFICE MANAGER my responsibilities include supervising six clerical staff and all personnel work (interviewing, hiring, disciplining and dismissing staff) for a total staff of 43. I also have total administrative control over advertising (current annual budget £5000 pa, sales, purchases, payroll and bookkeeping. The company's turnover is approximately £350,000. Notice required – 1 month.

1974–1980   Anytown Council Council
                                                    Anytown

I began work with the Anytown Council Council as CLERICAL ASSISTANT in the wages section. My duties included calculating wages/NI/PAYE/superannuation/additions and deductions for 230 employees as well as making up and distributing wage packets. In 1976 I was promoted to CLERICAL OFFICER in the finance section. My responsibilities included maintaining inventory records, organising and supervising the annual stocktake, preparing and checking purchase orders and processing payments and receipts.

Supplementary Information

I hold a full, clean, current driving licence and speak fluent French and some Spanish. I am currently attending a part-time 12-week course (evenings) in Modern Office Automation and Computerisation at the Anytown College of Further Education.

I am self-motivated, communicate well with people at all levels and feel that I have the drive, ability, qualifications and experience necessary to make a valuable contribution towards the development of your company.

Index